Twayne's United States Authors Series

Sylvia E. Bowman, *Editor*

INDIANA UNIVERSITY

Robert Benchley

ROBERT BENCHLEY

by **NORRIS W. YATES**

Iowa State University

(TUSAS) 138

Twayne Publishers, Inc.   ::   New York

MANUFACTURED IN THE UNITED STATES OF AMERICA BY
NATIONAL OFFSET, INC.
60 LAIGHT ST., NEW YORK, N. Y.

FOR BARBARA

Preface

It is a dangerous thing to attempt to analyze and describe the humor of any writer so that your audience will see that he is humorous. In fact, it is a dangerous thing to attempt to analyze humor at all. For, by the time you have taken a sentence and pointed out the humorous part and classified it and explained why it is humorous, it dies on you like a fish held too long out of water. And the chances are that the person to whom you have been explaining it won't think that it is funny anyway.[1]

WRITERS who examine humor like to quote such warnings before proceeding with their analyses. Robert Benchley's *caveat* has not deterred me from analyzing his humor as humor whenever such dissection contributes to the understanding of Benchley as a writer and of his place in the quickening current of American humor. Even when I think a piece not especially humorous, I have sometimes explained why it has been deemed so by other readers and how a certain idea or technique which stands out clearly in such a piece is basic, but perhaps less clear, in his other work.

In recent years, the written humor of Benchley has been overshadowed by that of James Thurber, E. B. White, and S. J. Perelman. But even if Benchley's humor were as dead as jokes made about the Redcoats during the Revolution, he would still be significant as an influence on younger humorists, including the three just named.[2] "Literary" humor—the humor of the familiar essay and of the sentimental short story, as distinguished from crackerbox humor, in which no pretense was made of being literary—went stale after Washington Irving, despite strenuous activity by Oliver Wendell Holmes; from about 1910 to 1930, however, an increasingly hectic era was reflected in the attempts of more and more writers, most of them with college or university backgrounds, to vivify the listless humor of the genteel tradition with stylistic leaven and satirical salt. Of these writers, Benchley was one of the best known and most effective.

In order to place him adequately in this stream of high-spirited highbrows, I have throughout the book documented the influence of other humorists on Benchley; I have also underlined his impact on editors, publishers, and other writers whenever I could without obscuring the discussion of Benchley's writing in and for itself.

The first chapter deals mainly with the acting, editing, drawing, and writing done by Robert while at Harvard; the second traces his subsequent attempts to find and to master a style and to break into print. Chapters 3 and 4 trace his rise to prominence as author and columnist, with space given to some of Benchley's ideas.

An analysis of Benchley's major themes and ideas, with emphasis on his recurrent contrasting of the bemused but good-hearted "Little Man" with the boobs, or mass-men, who surround and harass this character is the chief burden of Chapter 5. Chapter 6, a discussion of Benchley's theory and practice of humor, is a transition which leads into the more detailed examination of his humorous techniques in chapters 7, 8, and 9. The tenth and final chapter is devoted to Benchley's influence on other humorists, but this chapter has been foreshadowed by earlier material.

This book is about Benchley as a writer. His career in the movies has been slighted, as have been his excursions into radio, for both came too late to influence his writing very much. His roles as book reviewer, drama critic, and watchdog of the press (notably in "The Wayward Press" department of *The New Yorker*) have been summarized rather than analyzed. Because the book is a critical-analytical survey rather than a definitive study, some of Benchley's less significant experiments in humor, such as the series about a character named "Mr. Peters" which he did for *Redbook* magazine, have been neglected or barely mentioned; and his diction has been treated briefly and impressionistically (it awaits analysis, as does the language of American humor in general, by a qualified linguist armed possibly with a computer and certainly with a sense of humor).

This study is not a biography, and certain events in Benchley's life and background have been by-passed because they failed to throw more than merely speculative flickers of light on his writing. Most tempting were his mother's impulsive and quickly regretted wish that Robert rather than his elder brother had been killed in war, and the help given Robert, as well as the possessiveness shown concerning him, by his late brother's fiancée, without whose assistance the boy might never have enrolled at Exeter or at Harvard. Spasmodically ignored too have been Robert's close family ties in general, and his tangle of friendships with persons well known, less known, and unknown.

Iowa State University
Ames, Iowa

Norris W. Yates

Acknowledgments

I should like to thank the following for permission to quote from copyrighted material.

The Curtis Publishing Company for Robert C. Benchley, *Obiter Dicta*.

Harper and Row, Inc., for Robert Benchley, "Family Life in America" from *Love Conquers All*, and Robert Benchley, "Law-Breaking at Its Source" from *The Treasurer's Report*.

All other quotations from Benchley's books are used by permission of Mrs. Robert Benchley and are copyrighted © 1921, 1922, 1925, 1927, 1928, 1930, 1932, 1934, 1936, 1938, 1949, 1950, 1953.

I am grateful to the Harvard University Library for permission to examine part of the file of the Harvard *Lampoon*, to the Museum of Modern Art, in New York City, for allowing me to view the Benchley movies in its film library, and to Frank C. Strohkarck, of the Magazine Division, The Curtis Publishing Company, for assistance in procuring photocopies of those issues of *Obiter Dicta* edited by Benchley. I am especially grateful to Mrs. Gertrude D. (Mrs. Robert) Benchley for her guidance through the jungle of Benchley bibliography and for her assistance in obtaining photocopies of certain hard-to-get pieces by her late husband. I am also indebted to Mr. Nathaniel Benchley for his patience in answering many questions about his father, by letter and in person. Both of the individuals just named have also read the manuscript of this book and made many corrections of fact and helpful criticisms. Dr. Richard Gustafson, of Iowa State University, made stimulating suggestions about style; and my wife, Barbara, played a part in its making that can only be hinted at, here and in the dedication.

Final responsibility for all statements of fact and of evaluation in this book must, of course, be borne by the author alone.

Contents

Chronology

1865   Henry Weatherby Benchley, grandfather of Robert, re-
leased from jail in Texas, where he had reportedly been
lodged for working with the Underground Railroad.[1]

1889   Robert Charles Benchley born, Worcester, Massachusetts,
September 15, son of Charles Henry and Maria Jane
Moran Benchley.

1898   Edmund Nathaniel, older brother of Robert, killed in
Spanish-American War.

1904-   Attended high school in Worcester. Active in school
1907   drama club. Played as "super" (extra) with various road
companies when they performed in Worcester.

1907-   Enabled to enter Phillips Exeter Academy through finan-
1908   cial aid from Lillian Duryea, fiancée of Edmund. At
Exeter, belonged to Dramatic Club; did illustrations for
yearbook and literary magazine. As assignment in English
composition, wrote essay on embalming.

1908   Enrolled at Harvard, with financial help from Lillian
Duryea.

1909   Amplified Exeter essay on embalming. Began to draw
illustrations for Harvard *Lampoon*.

1910   Elected to Board of Editors of *Lampoon*, serving with
Frederick Lewis Allen and Gluyas Williams.

1910-   Improvised humorous oral monologues for club sessions.
1911   Taught Bible class at least once, with "penny ante limit."

1911   Acted in *The Crystal Gazer* (a "Hasty Pudding" show)
and in *Ralph Roister Doister*. Elected president of *Lampoon* editorial board, which included Frederick Lewis
Allen and Edward Streeter (future author of *Dere Mable*).

1912   Acted in *Below Zero* (a "Hasty Pudding" show). At Commencement, delivered traditionally humorous Ivy Oration. Bachelor of Arts degree withheld because of failure in one course. Worked briefly·for Boston Museum of Fine Art. October 17, started employment at Curtis Publishing Company.

1913   Received Bachelor of Arts from Harvard with Class of 1912. Began editing Curtis house organ, *Obiter Dicta*.

1914   Fired by Curtis, April 4. "Welfare secretary" for firm of paper mills in Boston. June 6, married Gertrude Darling whom he had known since childhood. First commercially published humorous piece, "Hints on Writing a Book," *Vanity Fair* (October, 1914). Organized boys' club for the Intercollegiate Social Service Committee at East Side House, a settlement unit; worked also with Urban League to improve Negro housing in Harlem.

1915   Upset Wardroom Club, an organization of naval officers, with speech purporting to announce reforms in Navy. By now, had considerable reputation as humorous monologuist. November 13, Nathaniel Goddard, his first child, born.

1916   Franklin P. Adams procured job for Benchley as reporter on New York *Tribune*. April 9, shifted to *The Tribune Magazine*, a Sunday supplement edited by Adams. Heywood Broun, George S. Kaufman, Irwin Edman, Deems Taylor, Arthur Folwell also on *Tribune* staff.

1917   Substituted for P. G. Wodehouse as drama critic for *Vanity Fair*. May 28, *The Tribune Magazine* discontinued. Twelve weeks as press agent for theatrical producer William A. Brady. Tried repeatedly and unsuccessfully to sell pieces to *Life*.

1918   January 3—May 4, aircraft news censor for Aircraft Board, Washington, D.C. In May, joined *The Tribune Graphic* (a forerunner of Sunday rotogravure sections). July 13, resigned because friend Ernest Gruening (later United States Senator from Alaska) was fired for allegedly pro-German views.[2] Worked for office of Liberty Loan.

1919   Upon suggestion by managing editor of *Collier's,* began series of home-life pieces with himself as "poor boob." May 19, managing editor of *Vanity Fair;* worked with Robert E. Sherwood and Dorothy Parker. Second son, Robert, born August 26.

1920   January 11, Dorothy Parker fired for criticism of Billie Burke (wife of Florenz Ziegfeld) and other show people. Benchley and Sherwood resigned next day. February 9, began column, "Books and Other Things," which ran three times weekly in the New York *World.* April 29, drama editor and columnist for *Life,* a job held until 1929. In May he became a home-owner in suburbia (Scarsdale).

1921   *Of All Things!* February 17, last column on "Books." March 4, signed to do weekly syndicated feature for David Lawrence. Allegedly took first drink of whisky.[3]

1922   *Love Conquers All.* April 30, delivered "The Treasurer's Report" in *No Sirree!,* amateur theatrical satire.

1923   First professional stage appearance: hired by Irving Berlin and Sam Harris to deliver "The Treasurer's Report" in the *Music Box Review,* Music Box Theater.

1925   *Pluck and Luck. The New Yorker* founded, February 21, 1925. December 19, first piece in *The New Yorker.*

1926   First movie job, writing subtitles for Raymond Griffith at Paramount

1927   *The Early Worm.* December 24, began feature under permanent head," The Wayward Press," for *The New Yorker,* under pseudonym "Guy Fawkes." Began drama department in *The Bookman.* Contributing editor of *Life.*

1928   *20,000 Leagues Under the Sea, or, David Copperfield.* Played lead in "The Treasurer's Report," first of forty-eight movie shorts in which he appeared.[4]

1929   Left *Life* to become drama columnist for *The New Yorker.*

1930   *The Treasurer's Report.*

1932   *No Poems.* Brief role in *Sport Parade,* first of many feature-length films in which he participated.

1933   June 12, began thrice-weekly column for King Features Syndicate.

1934   *From Bed to Worse.*

1935   "Oscar" from Academy of Motion Picture Arts and Sciences for writing and acting in best short film of year, *How to Sleep.*

1936   *My Ten Years in a Quandary.* August 14, terminated King Features column. Thereafter, did less writing of humor and more work for movies.

1938   *After 1903—What?*, first radio program.

1939   Last "Wayward Press" column, in *The New Yorker*, January 14.

1940   Last drama column, in *The New Yorker*, January 27.

1942   *Inside Benchley.*

1943   *Benchley Beside Himself.*

1945   Last film short, *I'm a Civilian Here Myself* (for U. S. Navy). November 21, died of cerebral hemorrhage.

1947   *Benchley—or Else!*

1949   *Chips Off the Old Benchley*, consisting largely of previously uncollected pieces.

1954   *The Benchley Roundup.* "The Doodlebugs," one of his earliest efforts, published, December, in Harvard *Lampoon.*

CHAPTER *1*

Humor at Harvard

THE humorous tale and essay in America were fertilized by jokebooks, almanacs, minstrel shows, early vaudeville, and the oral proverbs and yarns of the frontier. Less often stressed as an influence on American humor was the familiar essay as developed by Addison and Steele and perpetuated by *Punch* and other British comic periodicals. Recently, Hamlin Hill has called attention to yet another influence—nonsense humor. Nonsense was an important medium in Britain for Lewis Carroll, Edward Lear, and, later, A. A. Milne; and its redevelopment in North America by Gelett Burgess, Oliver Herford, Carolyn Wells, Stephen Leacock, and others marked a major difference between American humor of the nineteenth and the twentieth centuries.

Apparently it takes an educated man to write effective nonsense humor. Hill says of nonsense: "It carried whimsy to the verge of the irrational, and its importance in the line of development for modern humor lay precisely in its tendency to invert, to peer inward into a fantasy world, to play with language—always for fun, but in ways that provided a groundwork for later ramifications."[1] Such introspection along with a detachment that enabled the writer to explore his self-consciousness for fun and, above all, such tendency to play with words and phrases beyond the level of obvious punning—these have been attributes primarily of the educated writer; and, in the twentieth century, education has more and more often meant a college or university background. Stephen Leacock's "Gertrude had found her aunt in a syncope from which she passed into an apostrophe and never recovered"[2] was not the creation of a country editor but of a professor of political economy.

Whether or not recent American humorists write nonsense, many have done time on the campus and written for campus publications. College humor has yet to undergo detailed examination, but part of its influence on Robert Benchley may be traced.

I Crackerbarrel Humor and "Quality" Humor

At Harvard, Benchley wrote for two undergraduate periodicals: the serious *Advocate* and the humorous *Lampoon*. For the latter he drew many illustrations, and in his junior year (1911-1912) he served as its president. During these years at Harvard, American humor in magazines was still much as it had been in the last half of the previous century—rather sharply divided into "crackerbarrel" humor and into what one may call "genteel" or "literary" humor. The former was characterized by dialect, misspellings, odd constructions of phrase and sentence, epigrams, and an attitude of contempt or indifference toward formal education and toward "correct," copybook style. The general impression conveyed was that this type of humor emanated from a shrewd but uneducated fellow who dispensed his homely truths to a circle of loafers around the crackerbarrel or the pot-bellied stove in a country store. Popular crackerbarrel humorists between the Civil War and World War I included Artemus Ward, Petroleum Vesuvius Nasby, Orpheus C. Kerr, Josh Billings, Bill Nye, and, latest and best, Mr. Dooley (Finley Peter Dunne).

Genteel humorists tended to use the "highfalutin'" language rejected by the crackerbox oracles and to specialize in learned allusions and deft word-play. Above all other literary humorists in reputation stood Oliver Wendell Holmes, largely because of *The Autocrat of the Breakfast-Table* (1858) and three later books in a similar style.[3] In the 1890's, the liveliest of the literary humorists were John Kendrick Bangs and Eugene Field; and Bangs confessed that he created the title character of *The Idiot* (1895) "with *The Autocrat* in one hand."[4] Even in their occasional self-mockery, these writers worked within the high-collar style used by Holmes:

> I am willing—I said—to exercise your ingenuity in a rational and contemplative manner.—No, I do not proscribe certain forms of philosophical speculation which involve an approach to the absurd or the ludicrous, such as you may find, for example, in the folio of the Reverend Father Thomas Sanchez, in his famous Disputations, *De Sancto Matrimonio.*[5]

Despite several similarities of the crackerbarrel tradition to the bookish tradition in humor, the line between them remained sharp even when the two styles were used, as they often were, by the same writer. In fact, a standard device for achieving incongruity was the frame tale, or tale within a tale. In the framework, the authorial "I" described the crackerbox character and related the circumstances of their meeting. Thus Holmes, in the person of a journalist, opens and closes a piece about the Autocrat's landlady with an account of his visit to her in quest of information; the middle part of the piece is a monologue in dialect by the landlady.[6]

Sometimes the writer, when using the high style in the framework, unwittingly fell into the pompousness or sentimentality which he mocked in his other capacity of unlettered rustic. Bret Harte often displayed this discrepancy, and E. W. Townsend could write, behind the mask of "Chimmie Fadden," the newsboy-philosopher, " 'De mug was no dude, I could tell dat' "; and he could then, in another piece, come out quite seriously, as a literate editor, with, "I felt that my popularity was as firmly fixed in that camp as the broad foundation of its mighty mountains towering in everlasting serenity."[7] Individually as well as collectively, American humorists followed two divergent tracks and consequently made little headway on either.

II   *Crackerboxers, Columnists, and College Men*

However, there were signs that the two streams of humor might eventually mingle instead of exist separately, side by side. One sign was the frequency with which they did exist, literally, side by side: a typical page in *Puck* at the turn of the century includes an attack in dialect on the Democratic Party, and a cartoon featuring the "Gibson girl," one of the favorite archetypes of genteel humor.[8] All three of the leading comic weeklies, *Puck*, *Judge*, and *Life*, as well as the leading comic monthly, *Vanity Fair*, accepted numerous contributions both from the crackerbarrel writers and their more polished brethren. The two volumes of *Life* for 1912 contain quips or pieces by such composers of literate light verse as Franklin P. Adams, Arthur Guiterman, Wallace Irwin, Carolyn Wells, Deems Taylor (not yet a composer of music), and Oliver Herford; these volumes also include cultivated prose by such writers as E. S. Martin, Thomas L. Masson, James Metcalf, J. B. Kerfoot (all on the staff of *Life*), and Agnes Repplier. Not to be confused with the magazine founded in 1936 by Henry Luce, *Life* was first published in 1883 by a group of university graduates headed by John Ames Mitchell (Harvard) and John Kendrick Bangs (Columbia)—both fresh from work on their respective collegiate publications. But in 1912, *Life* was still hospitable to the work of Robert J. Burdette (the "Burlington *Hawkeye* Man") and to other merchandise from the crossroads store. Crackerbarrel humor also kept company with "quality" humor in the departments reserved for lighter material by *Harper's*, the *Century*, and the *Bookman*.

Probably more important than what was happening in the magazines was the proliferation of the informal column of opinion and chat in the big-city daily newspapers. The new type of personal columnist appealed to the growing masses of urban readers who might or might not be university men and who probably read the crackerbox columns of Mr. Dooley and "Abe Martin." Yet they also liked some of the humor in school-book English by writers who made sympathetic use of literary, artistic, and historical background. Of course, copybook English could not be dull *and* humorous, and the new columnists tended to vitalize their college-level diction and their erudition with a chattiness and pithiness like that of the crackerbarrel sages.

Bert Leston Taylor began one of the earliest of these columns in 1900—"A Line-o'-Type or Two," for the Chicago *Tribune*. Taylor was "urbane, civilized, a little aloof"; but he could refer to a " 'quiet wedding' " as "unmarred by the usual screams of the bridegroom."[9] Another Chicago columnist, Keith Preston, translated Horace wittily, as did a disciple of Taylor, Franklin P. Adams ("F.P.A."). Adams began his first column on the Chicago *Journal* in 1903, moved it to the New York *Evening Mail* 1904-1913), and then took it to the *Tribune* of that city, where it was first called "The Conning Tower."

Of the "light" columnists who became active between 1900 and World War I, Adams had the most influence on his fellow humorists. Benchley declared that "In F.P.A. we find a combination which makes it possible for us to admit our learning and still be held honorable men," and younger writers cut some of their teeth by contributing to Adams' column, including a yet unknown James Thurber who in 1926 did an entire issue of "The Conning Tower."[10]•

In 1912, the year Benchley left Harvard, Heywood Broun began "It Seems to Me" for the New York *Tribune;* and Don Marquis started "The Sun Dial" for the New York *Sun,* a column he soon began to pepper with pieces about a rich flapper named Hermione and with free verse about a cockroach named Archy. Meanwhile "The Patient Observer" (Simeon Strunsky) had been writing "Post-Impressions" in the New York *Post* since 1904; Christopher Morley had begun a department for the Philadelphia *Public Ledger* in 1910, and down in Baltimore, H. L. Mencken had started "Knocks and Jollies" in the *Herald* (1903). In 1911, Mencken sharpened the "Free Lance" in the *Evening Sun.*

While no *necessary* relation may have existed between university training and the rise of urbane humor in the personal column, still a partial correlation did exist. George Ade had a Bachelor of Science degree from Purdue, but developed a slangy, pithy crackerbarrel style in his column for the Chicago *Record,* "Stories of the Streets and of the Town" (1893-1900); Mencken's learning had been acquired on no campus and Adams had stayed barely a year at the University of Michigan. On the other hand, Morely was a Rhodes Scholar; Broun attended Harvard for four years; and Bert Leston Taylor went into journalism from the College of the City of New York. Of the new humorists who developed their talent in writing for campus publications, Bangs had earned a name as the "great College Vituperator" on the *Acta Columbiana* in 1882-1883,[11] Gelett Burgess edited the magazine *Tech* at Massachusetts Institute of Technology, and Strunsky lifted the *Columbia Monthly* to a nearly professional level before he was graduated in 1900. Among those in the next generation, James Thurber edited the *Sun-Dial* magazine at Ohio State before he left that university in 1919, and E. B. White edited the Cornell *Daily Sun* before his graduation in 1921.

III   *Benchley and the "Lampoon"*

A rising standard of education and growth in the number of university-trained humorists and readers was, therefore, changing styles in American humor.[12] And Benchley's four years as a Harvard Yard-bird played a role in his development as a humorist. Benchley was elected to the editorial board of the *Lampoon* in the spring of 1910 and became president early in 1911, relinquishing his post about a year later. During his tenure, he worked with a crew of humorists who mutually stimulated one another. Other writers and cartoonists for the *Lampoon* who later contributed to the swelling current of suave humor in commercial periodicals included Gluyas Williams—the illustrator of all of Benchley's books—and Frederick Lewis Allen, who wrote a number of pieces about bewildered little men baffled by sports, ladies, and the problem of communicating with their fellowmen ("Rupert had always felt himself peculiarly helpless and inept."[13] He was, too.). Edward Laurence McKinney, Laurence Redway, and Paul Hollister also published humor later on, as a sideline to careers in other fields; and Edward Streeter scored a popular success with *Dere Mable: Love Letters of a Rookie*—which, however, was crackerbox material in its use of dialect and of a shrewd but ignorant commentator.

Other board members who became authors of distinction included Roger Burlingame (*The March of the Iron Men*, etc.) and John Reed, whom Benchley recalled as one radical who differed from the sour-puss stereotypes of proletarian drama in that he "smiled now and then and even cracked jokes, and did not always enter a room as if they [sic] were the man coming to take away the piano."[14] Much has been made of the presence at Harvard during these years of Professors Josiah Royce, George Santayana, Ralph Barton Perry, Charles T. Copeland, Francis J. Child, and George Lyman Kittredge, and of future literati such as T. S. Eliot and Walter Lippmann (both of the class of 1910), E.E. Cummings ('15), and John Dos Passos ('16). Perhaps not enough has been said of the less ponderous talent associated with the *Lampoon*.

During the years of Benchley's involvement, the *Lampoon* was published twenty times a year in issues of about thirty pages each. A fourth to a third of each number consisted of display advertising, segregated mostly in the front and back portions of the magazine. Advertisers included clothing stores, custom tailors, bookstores, publishers, student-supply shops, gift shops, restaurants, and (surprisingly, perhaps, in that time of creeping prohibition) distillers of wines and hard liquors. The general impression conveyed by the advertisement sections is one of costly modishness, like the advertising in the *Smart Set, Vanity Fair,* and later in *The New Yorker.*

Roughly a third to a half of the remaining space was used for humorous illustrations; only a third to a quarter of the total space was available for prose and verse, and some of that space was occupied by the one or two editorials, which tended to be serious or only faintly humorous in tone. Much of the prose humor consisted of brief jokes and anecdotes, often in dialogue form. The occasional narrative or essay was rarely as long as five hundred words. Among the essays and poems were quite a few parodies, mostly of popular authors or of classroom lecturers. At least one student tried his hand at imitating the fables in slang of George Ade, but English that would have merited a good grade in composition classes was far more frequent than slang or dialect. "Lampy" had definitely turned its back on the crackerbox idiom. The over-all effect of the magazine was of a periodical trying hard to be both humorous and respectable.

Much of the humor, of course, was topical and concerned dull lecturers, burdensome routines of study, horse-play in the dorms, club activities, dating, high times in Cambridge or Boston, and the superiority of Harvard over Yale. Such topicality tends in general to set campus humor apart from that of the rest of the world, and in this respect the *Lampoon* was no exception. Moreover, the *Lampoon* at that time undertook no crusades and brandished no torches about burning issues within the Yard, although Robert, as a person, was easily aroused by any obvious injustice or clear-cut social problem. In its uniform blandness the magazine also belied its title: there were few lampoons in this periodical.

Once in a while somebody's high spirits erupted in a forerunner of the present-day "sick" joke. One such joke concerned a guest who brushed his teeth with a "tooth-powder" that turned out to be the remains of the hostess' "poor Aunt Mary."[15] On the whole, however, the *Lampoon* resembled *Vanity Fair* in sticking mainly to light satire of manners and to coterie humor.

Benchley drew for the *Lampoon* more than he wrote: the score for 1909 through 1912 is, drawings, 71; prose pieces, 23, not including nine more essays on which he collaborated.[16] As an artist he was undistinguished; there is more interest in the captions. The collegian from Worcester was fond of punning;

his first drawing in the *Lampoon* showed two Irishwomen standing by a garbage can, and one is saying, "Ain't it offal, Mabel?" In another Benchley drawing, a policeman asks a lady who has fallen in the street, "Did you have vertigo?"; and she replies, "No, only about two blocks." Other philological convulsions include "Frieze for a Yard Room," in which students shiver under a ceiling draped with icicles, and "An Organ Recital," in which a lecturer gestures with a pointer before an anatomical chart.[17] Puns are much less common in the "rough" or cracker-barrel tradition of humor than in the suave or 'smooth" tradition ("i konsider punning a sort ov literary prostitushun in which future happynesz iz swopped oph for the plezzure ov the moment," said Josh Billings[18]); and, except for their feebleness, Benchley's puns in the *Lampoon* show him heading into the urban and urbane tradition rather than back toward the crossroads.

As a collegian, Benchley could also try the non-sequitur, another technique not unknown to the crackerbox philosophers but much more common among the nonsense writers within the "smooth" tradition. "What is wrong with this picture," he asked about a drawing that included a farmer with his head sketched upside down and a horse with human front feet. The second line of the caption is, "Yesterdays answer——The man had no liver."[19]

The subject-matter of the drawings does suggest Benchley's early preoccupation with certain themes that crop up later in his work. One strip shows the mutual irritation of a student and an elderly relative with the inappropriate Christmas present each has received from the other. Another drawing parodies the absurd plots of typical melodrama; another scoffs at "Plans for the New Germanic Museum." Cartoons with political implications include jibes at the Harvard "Anarchist League" and "Atheist Society" and at the woman suffrage movement.[20] The drama was, first and last, a major field of interest for Benchley; and abuses of the Christmas spirit, as well as pedantry in science, were to be important targets for his satire—satire marked by a true middle-roader's distrust of extremism in religion or politics.

IV *The Student as "Little Man"*

Generally speaking, the most important feature of Benchley's humor was a character-type which may be labeled the "Little

Man." In the nineteenth century, John Phoenix, Charles Heber Clark, and others had sometimes depicted gentle, bewildered fumblers trying unsuccessfully to cope with an environment too big and too complex for them. Such types among Mark Twain's protagonists included "the Sufferer," "the Simpleton," and "the Tenderfoot"; these labels, assigned them by John Gerber, describe them.[21] In his papers on "the Idiot" (1893-1917), John Kendrick Bangs created a broker's clerk who was so quick-witted and sensible that his companions thought him slow-witted and foolish—a "wise fool," wearing a white collar in an urban rather than a rural environment. Stephen Leacock, whose influence Benchley generously acknowledged, evolved a meek middle-class character who was so scared by the atmosphere of a bank that he asked for his fifty-six dollars "in fifties" and the remainder in sixes."[22] Leacock's little man in *Literary Lapses* (1910) was much like Benchley's ten years later: he spoke college-level English, had a white-collar job and a modest income, and lived in a respectable flat, or, more often, in the suburbs. Most important, he was mentally disturbed but never quite lost his moral sense.

Between 1910 and 1919, while Benchley was painfully developing a style that included the mask of the Little Man, Irvin S. Cobb was impersonating a comic fat man at the mercy of doctors and other agents of civilization,[23] and A. A. Milne in Britain was writing about a mild-mannered suburbanite who was baffled by the simplest mechanical devices, such as a geological hammer, the nib of his pen, and his squeaky collar.[24] In developing his own Milquetoast-Bumstead figure, Benchley was joining and augmenting a trend.

Doubtless, Benchley had no intention of making it easy for scholars to categorize him as a humorist of the Little Man; his type-figure was an expression of his own character, only slightly exaggerated. After three years of manual training in high school, Benchley still couldn't drive a nail without bending it; and later, on a movie set, his bumbling drew from a carpenter the remark, "My God, he's a born one—he does it without thinking!"[25] The trend toward this sort of humor, however, helped Benchley's variety of it to "take" with Yard audiences and later with readers of *Vanity Fair*, *Life*, *The New Yorker*, and other periodicals for the literate. His talk, "Through the Alimentary Canal with Gun and Camera," reduced the staid Harvard Club of Boston to a "quivering shambles," and his other oral travelogue given as an incompetent, gentle, but "quietly-pleased-with-himself explorer" drew so many requests for repeats from his fellow students that he alternated it with a take-off on a politician, of which his son Nathaniel says, "It does not take an acute analyst to spot the style that blossomed out in the Treasurer's Report, some ten or twelve years later.[26]

Robert's little man appears as a professor of history in the *Lampoon* (LXI, May 24, 1911, 188). Delivering a lecture on "The Alphabetical Aspects of Slavery, regarded in the Light of Hereditary Rheumatism," he pontificates: "Now the first thing to observe is that, in general, the slaves in the South, previous to 1848, were almost entirely men, women, or children." At the Commencement exercises for the Class of 1912, Benchley gave the Ivy Oration, a humorous speech which was a traditional part of the Class Day rites.[27] Several techniques which he used more deftly later are practiced in it with the laboriousness found in much student humor:

Surprise is not the name for the emotion with which I am overcome at being just now suddenly called upon to address you. It is nothing short of confusion. Nothing could have been farther from my thoughts as I sat listening to the other speakers here this afternoon, than that my modest voice should be desired to lend a touch of dignity to this occasion. Why a quarter of an hour ago I was sitting in my room, looking for a position for next year, when the Bursar, that Prince of Good Fellows, that Shylock of Melancholy Dane, came bounding up the stairs, and laying a sympathetic hand on my shoulder said, "Bob, old man, aren't you coming down to say a few words to the Big Red Team? The boys are all calling for you down there." Then it all came over me like a flask—this was Class Day! I did remember having seen a program of the week, in which, somewhere between ball-games with Yale and Phi Beta Kappa Exhibits there was made casual mention of a Class Day exercise, but I understood that it was to be held only in case the ball-game at New Haven was called off on account of rain, and besides, I really did not dare to leave the Yard, for fear lest I had not the right colored ticket, and that, once out, I could never get back in again to get my clean clothes for the summer vacation. So here it was Class Day, and there I was in my room hemming napkins. Quickly I drew on a pair of shoes and my cap and gown, and breaking into a run—and a perspiration, soon found myself, unless I am mistaken, here.

Laboriousness aside, several techniques used in this opening paragraph were practiced by both crackerbox and white-collar humorists. The lecture-monologue form used in parody of itself has already been noted. Basic, too, is self-kidding, another crucial device in the lectures of Artemus Ward, Mark Twain, and Stephen Leacock. The scrambling of items from Shakespeare had precedent in *Huckleberry Finn* as well as in genteel humor, and so did the use of anti-climax (in the last word of the paragraph).

Bumptiously imagining oneself to be the right-hand man of a great personage was a device favored mainly by the crackerboxers: Jack Downing and Sut Lovingood had claimed to be advisors to Andrew Jackson and to "Abe Linkhorn," respectively; and Mr. Dooley referred to Admiral Dewey as "Cousin George Dooley" and to President McKinley as "me frind Mack."[28] On the other hand, puns and the faulty parallelism of dissimilar items ("breaking into a run—and a perspiration") were employed mostly by the more genteel players with language. The same was true of nonsense, of which the superfluous "unless I am mistaken" is a weak example and so is the notion that one may look for a job by sitting in one's room (a better sample later in the speech concerns the "election and inauguration of Sam White as President and Fellows of Princeton").

How flagrant must a non-sequitur be in order to lapse into nonsense? Having asked the question, let us dodge it for the moment. Meanwhile—any sudden change of subject, any rupture of a sequence of thought, if that rupture be illogical and irrelevant, is here considered a non-sequitur. To be humorous, it must also be unexpected and strikingly inappropriate.

The scrambling of allusions and the use of faulty parallelism are really but variations of the non-sequitur, and the use of aimless digression may often be thought of as the same basic device in less extreme form. The Ivy Oration is certainly digressive: the orator announces that his speech will concern the "Malefactors of Great Health" (a few sons of the magnates charged by Teddy Roosevelt with being "malefactors of great wealth" were doubtless among the audience), great issues of the day within the Yard, and "the Social Usurpation of our Colleagues." In his subsequent rambling, the orator skirted the first two topics and announced his omission of the third. Occasionally his wanderings took turns abrupt enough to be called nonsensical: thus he labeled his second topic, supposedly on university issues, as "Oration Proper—Section A, under the General Heading of Cotton Goods and Steel Rails." A little later he said:

> It is with the customary Class Day mingled emotions of pleasure and regret that we bask here today, and with eyes dimmed by Boylston St. dust look back over the seventeen pre-digested courses that have constituted our educational banquet. Let us ponder ponderously on these things. What have we accomplished? What new visions have we seen? When and why does all this mean? O, Brothers, we are all unthinking in this extremity. We have waited and the innumerable caravan has gone without us. We have sung and the echo has not come back. And now I ask you, what has the Republican party ever done for you—the working man?

Like the speech as a whole, the passage is a parody of the murky prose that hovers like darkness visible over the platform on commencement days and other public occasions. The word-play, the misuse in parallel of "when and why,"[29] and the non-sequitur are all ways of forcibly joining incongruous contexts and thereby enhancing the disorganized effect of the piece.

V "Goons" and "Jiggers"

The Ivy Oration shows which way Benchley was headed, but it also shows that he had not yet advanced beyond the limitations of collegiate humor. It is concerned, ·quite naturally, with matters of student interest; it is wordy; it shows a straining for effect, as in "ponder ponderously." Robert's pieces for the *Lampoon* have the same defects, despite deft foreshadowings like the reference to spring as heralded by "the plaintive cry of the mating earthworms" (LXI, April 13, 1911, 127). To use the terminology of his friend Frederick Lewis Allen, Benchley was still a "goon" rather than the "jigger" he later became. "A goon is a person with a heavy touch as distinguished from a jigger, who has a light touch. While jiggers look on life with a genial eye, goons take a more stolid and literal view.... What they lack is the playful mind."[30] George Washington, James Fenimore Cooper, and Warren G. Harding (said Allen) were "goons"; Lincoln, Lytton Strachey, and Lloyd-George belonged to the other tribe. When it came down to sitting and writing out his humor, Benchley lost some of his playfulness, and the editor of *Collier's* probably had the heaviness of Robert's touch in mind when he rejected some of the young writer's pieces as "too collegiate."[31]

As an undergraduate, Benchley showed signs of broadening the range of his humor when he edited an entire number of the *Lampoon* (LXI, March 3, 1911) as a parody of *Life*. The best bit of writing in this issue was a collaboration of Benchley and E. L. McKinney entitled "The Harvard Lampoon Sewing Circle" (153), a question-and-answer department which was mostly farcical parodies of recipes and of "How to Do It" recommendations for the home. Once parody in this column crosses the line into pure nonsense, in the instructions for making "lingerie shoe-strings." The final instruction concerns "the application of the lingerie, which can easily be done between courses at dinner by simply taking the lingerie and applying it to the shoe-strings." The self-conscious suggestiveness is another mark of collegiate humor. When the later Benchley chose on rare occasions to become suggestive, he did so without the snigger.

Apparently referring to Benchley's entanglement in disorganized trivia, William Miller has written that "he seems to have raised the *Weltanschauung* of the college humor magazine to a way of life."[32] A *Weltanschauung* is not easy to find in the *Lampoon* of 1909-1912, but after leaving the Harvard Yard, Benchley tried to develop an amused detachment toward life there or in any other locale—a detachment suggesting a well-stocked but disorganized mind being laughed at by the better part of itself. In writing college or "company" humor, he also tried later to emphasize its implications for the world at large. A piece written during his most successful years, "What College Did to Me,"[33] conveys a feeling that the chaos of the curriculum and the confusion of the student were part of a wider problem: a misconception about college which was shared alike by students and by the general public. He laughs at that "part of the American Credo that all the college student learns is to catch punts and dance," and he implies that students, their financial backers, and their instructors cultivate a vague complacency about one's chance to learn a great deal (of trivia) in the college classroom.

Even in retrospect, Benchley seldom tried to satirize his university background as a whole, but he was effective in focusing on single facets of university life and in investing his satire with hints that went beyond the campus or Yard. "The King of Razbo-Jazbo" and "The Musical Clubs' Concert"—contributed to *College Humor*—were lively parodies of college glee clubs and of the Harvard Hasty Pudding shows, respectively; but they could also be taken as satires of community singing or of musical comedies in general. "Back to the Game," written from the viewpoint of an alumnus disillusioned about his own behavior, showed a good deal of detachment and little of the overly eager junior who had been absorbed in Yard matters. Perhaps Benchley was still laying the ghost of this former undergraduate when, in 1936, he criticized *Brother Rat* for being "very Brown-of-Harvard-and-Stover-at-Yale" and admonished the former college men in the audience for giving "an air of Hasty Pudding to the evening which grew more and more oppressive as the night wore on."[34]

The most important raw material of his humor Robert Benchley had brought with him to Cambridge. An alumnus reminisced, "You could tell Bench was bound to go places from his first days at Harvard. He kept his classmates doubled up with laughter."[35] However, during his four years within the Yard, Robert developed his talent for improvising oral monologues and for delivering this humor with a deadly solemn countenance. What he yet lacked was a closer view of the world at large and the skill of the professional writer. Several years of apprenticeship lay between Benchley and success as a humorous essayist, but he had begun that apprenticeship at the university.

Learning the Craft

A FTER leaving Harvard, Benchley did not quite starve in a garret; but seven lean years passed before he had built up enough reputation as a writer through free-lancing to get a position that meant a steady, decent salary for writing pretty much as he pleased. Between 1912, when he left Cambridge, and 1919, when he took over the managing-editorship of *Vanity Fair*, he got and lost jobs as publicity writer and editor, secretary, "adman," reporter, press agent, and bureaucratic propagandist. In his spare time he tried to write pieces of which he need not be ashamed but which would, nonetheless, sell.

His ideals of excellence during this period may be suggested by his daydreams about starting "a *real* humor magazine—one that would be independent of advertisers, and that would include stuff by Stephen Leacock, Rea Irvin, Homer Croy, Franklin P. Adams, Gelett Burgess, and others of their caliber"[1]—men who wrote or drew in the careful but seemingly casual vein that later became identified with *The New Yorker*. Nathaniel Benchley says of his father that, "In his determination to write something Really Good, he kept a notebook, in which he entered ideas, thoughts, phrases, and descriptions, more or less as they occurred to him."[2] Even in his apparently indolent moments, Robert Benchley was working on his writing.

I *Hack Work*

One of Robert's brief jobs was helping Richard Walsh (later the husband of Pearl Buck) prepare most of the copy for *Obiter Dicta*, a new house organ for employees of the Curtis Publishing Company. The first issue was criticized by the management as "too technical, too scattering, and wholly lacking in punch"[3];

and the criticism was, on the whole, just. Benchley could not make himself do good hack work. Here and there in *Obiter Dicta* one can detect a straining at the leash. One department of the magazine, entitled "Till Forbidden: a Depository for Incoherent Copy," included a series of "Publicity Playlets" in which various absurdities in advertising were burlesqued. Though not much above the level of *Lampoon* humor, these playlets foreshadowed Benchley's later nonsense humor. For example:

ACT I

TIME: 1885

PLACE: Early morning in the textile market.

Curtain rises on a broad field.
Wealthy but honest Manufacturer discovered alone in the center of the stage, silently manufacturing Textiles.
(Business of clicking looms.)
Enter—Chorus of Retailers (slowly).
They cluster about the wealthy but honest Manufacturer, holding out money. Slowly and silently he exchanges it for Woolen Stuffs.
Enter—Mob of Consumers who stand expectantly behind a Rock until joined by the Chorus of Retailers with the Goods.
Exit—Retailers and Consumers, bargaining.
Manufacturer lights a Cigar and continues silently to manufacture Textiles.

(Curtain)

ACT II

TIME: 1913

PLACE: High noon in the textile market.

Curtain rises on a teeming mart.
Handsome young Textile Manufacturer discovered manufacturing Textiles on a raised platform above the heads of the Mob of Consumers who stand watching with evident interest.
Enter—Chorus of Retailers, running and carrying Cash-Registers. They are hailed loudly by the Mob of Consumers and are pushed by them up to where the Handsome Young Textile Manufacturer is conspicuously, yet undeniably, manufacturing textiles. Business of buying and selling.

Through a break in the crowd the Wealthy but Honest Manufacturer is momentarily seen manufacturing textiles silently and
unnoticed behind a Stump. Crowd closes up again and he is
seen no more.
General cheering and waving of goods and money.

(Curtain)

TABLEAU: Spirit of Advertising placing a wreath of Berries
on the head of the Handsome Young Manufacturer with one
hand, beckons with the other to the Wealthy but Honest Manufacturer to come out from behind the Stump.

(Curtain)[4]

The second and third of these playlets likewise have some of
the quirkiness that would enliven Benchley's best essays. In
"No. 2: A Comedy in Too Many Acts," a King who merely wants
to spend money plans a grandiose advertising campaign, suddenly decides to economize, and pays his engraver with "a
nickel and a cross-town transfer." The engraver puts the nickel
in his pocket, eats the transfer, and says, "God help the poor
Sailors on a Night like this." The campaign flops, allegedly because the engraver made cheap plates; and the King's reaction,
like that of Lewis Carroll's Duchess, is "Off with his Head!"
In the third skit, a salesman induces a proprietor to stock his
general store with "Prepared Welsh Rarebits," with the result
that "They sat on my Shelves, and sat on my Shelves, and when
the Winter had gone and the Spring came they multiplied on
me—once—twice—and then Considerable. Millions of young Ones
came and ate up all the rest of my Stock. They over-ran my
living-room and nibbled at my Little Daughter."[5] The excessive
capitalization suggests Ade's fables, and the action has overtones
of Ellis Parker Butler's *Pigs Is Pigs* (1906); but Butler is typically in the crackerbox vein when he merely exaggerates a real
phenomenon—the fecundity of guinea pigs.
Benchley is more like Lardner and Perelman in crossing the
invisible line from mere exaggeration into fantasy connected with
reality only by the free association of words. What originally
sent Benchley into the wild blue was undoubtedly the associa-

tion of "rarebit" with "rabbit" and "rat," even as the entirely correct grammatical association of "out of" with place, as well as with condition, enabled Lardner to have fun in "I Gaspiri" with

FIRST STRANGER   Where was you born?

SECOND STRANGER   Out of wedlock.

FIRST STRANGER   That's a mighty pretty country
around there.[6]

Likewise, the ease with which one may associate the verb "spread" with other verbs of movement results in ,Perelman's "The melody spread rapidly up Fifth Avenue, debouched into Broadway, detoured into Park, and soon the entire city was humming the infectious strain."[7]

Free association of words is basic in much humor that is not nonsense and in many devices of "serious" prose and poetry, but Benchley was one of the earlier Americans to use it for nonsense purposes. And in these capers that enlivened his hack work, he unintentionally kicked higher than he would for several years in his more ambitious attempts to be amusing.[8]

Most of *Obiter Dicta* was given over to such features as "The Farmer-Businessman," "Sex Education" (vaguely commending gestures made toward this goal by the *Ladies' Home Journal*), "Intensive Typography," "Censorship," "From Cider-Press to Rotary," "Sentiment in Business," "Cultivating the Jobber," "Trademark Pitfalls," and "Selling $300,000,000 Worth." Within a year the Curtis company decided that Robert was not happy in his job. The company was right.

Benchley was a rebel, but not in the fashion of Thoreau, the Greenwich Village bohemians, or the expatriates. During the 1920's, his job as drama reviewer often brought him out in white tie, tuxedo, and top hat; and no one loved an impromptu party better than he. Nevertheless, he was a family man who read Dickens' *A Christmas Carol* every year to his two sons; and once he told Thurber that he didn't believe in second marriages.[9] He also didn't believe in alcohol, until the challenge of Prohibition. However, his revolt against deadening routine, overweening authority, crass commercialism, conformity for conformity's sake, and pretense of all kinds broke out continually, in print and in action. The bits of satire in *Obiter Dicta* were rebellious twitches; so, too, may one account for the practical jokes that Benchley played from time to time throughout his career. At the annual convention of the Curtis people, he put on a red wig, false beard, and eyeglasses; represented himself as Mr. Constantine, the president of a Seattle advertising agency; and delivered a tirade against certain practices of the Curtis firm. Cyrus H. K. Curtis "had to be forcibly restrained from jumping to his feet,"[10] but Robert got away with his criticisms by ripping off his disguise and closing with a chorus of "Heaven Will Protect the Working Girl."

Perhaps feeling that he could easily be spared at the home office, Benchley's bosses at Curtis sent him from time to time on trips to survey some particular business process, such as the merchandising of gingham or of pianolas; and many years later Benchley, in "The Woolen Mitten Situation,"[11] parodied the sort of reports they wanted concerning these trips. "The Curtis publications—their names escape me at the moment"—got no glory in restrospect, but at least these trips gave Benchley some of the wide knowledge of business he showed later when he hooked banderillos into Babbittry.

II *Heaven and the Working Journalist*

From Curtis, Robert went to a job with a firm of Boston paper mills, as a hybrid of publicity man and welfare worker. At about the time his employers abolished this job, Franklin P. Adams, who did the column "The Conning Tower" in the New York *Tribune*, found a place for Benchley as reporter on the "Trib" and, three months later, as a feature writer for a new Sunday supplement to that newspaper. On the Sunday staff, Benchley worked under Adams and with Arthur Folwell, a former editor of *Puck;* and he also saw something of Heywood Broun, George S. Kaufman, Deems Taylor, and Irwin Edman who were also on the *Tribune*.[12] The mutually friendly association of these urbane, learned, and lively workers in prose is noteworthy.

Significant also in Robert's humor was a moral zeal, derived perhaps from his New England background and from his crusading family. Some had been active in the Underground Railroad, a grandfather had spent time in a Texas jail, and Robert's mother was a fanatical "dry."[13] This urge to do good, outstanding in Benchley even during the era of Woodrow Wilson and of the Progressive party, caused him to worry continually about whether his writing was helping the cause of progress, and led him to do settlement work with a New York City boys' club. It also cost him two jobs. After a stint in wartime Washington as a censor for the secretive Aircraft Board, he went back to the New York *Tribune;* but, when his friend Ernest Gruening (later United States Senator from Alaska) was fired as managing editor because of unfounded allegations that he was pro-German, Robert resigned, despite concern for the wife and child he himself was by then supporting.[14]

Two years later, Benchley, its then managing editor, and Robert E. Sherwood quit *Vanity Fair* because Dorothy Parker had been fired for her criticisms of various show people, especially of Billie Burke, the actress-wife of producer Florenz Ziegfeld. Nathaniel Benchley has stated that his father was, in a non-denominational way, a deeply religious man—a trait not easy to infer from Robert's humor—but Heaven did not protect these working journalists, nor did Benchley expect it to. Whatever his feelings about the next world, he knew from experience that this world was an absurd mess, not the least of its absurdities being the tendency of some people, himself among them, to obey a conscience that did not make cowards of them.

III   Humorous "Voices," 1910-1920

Reviewing Wallace Irwin's *Letters of a Japanese Schoolboy* (1909), John Macy declared,

> It is a long, long time between true satirists. There will never be another Dooley. There will never be another Togo [the Japanese schoolboy-philosopher]. The next satirist, who will be due in about ten years, will have difficulty in finding a voice and a lingo equal to those of Mr. Dooley and Mr. Togo as a vehicle for comment upon current events and the old, old human foibles.[15]

Macy's prophetic eye was sharp. During the second decade of the century, no one humorist or satirist stood out as George Ade and Finley Peter Dunne had in the first.

However, plenty of young talent was active. Among the news-paper columnists, "F. P. A.," Don Marquis, Heywood Broun ("It Seems to Me"), Simeon Strunsky ("The Patient Observer"), Christopher Morley, Kin Hubbard, and Bert Leston Taylor had large and growing followings; H. L. Mencken attracted attention from 1911 until 1915 when his department in the Baltimore *Evening Sun* had been dropped because of his pro-German views. In 1913, Ring Lardner took over a sporting column, "In the Wake of the News," for the Chicago *Tribune* and in it developed the style that made him famous. Among the mass magazines, the *Saturday Evening Post* and *Collier's* furnished a hospitable market for humorous fiction, including that of Lardner, Irvin S. Cobb, Montague Glass with his Jewish comedians Potash and Perlmutter, and Harry Leon Wilson, who moved into the *Post* with the serials *Bunker Bean* and *Ruggles of Red Gap*.

In the more rarified air of the quality periodicals, the *Century* and *Harper's* maintained departments of humor: respectively, "In a Lighter Vein" and "The Lion's Mouth." Humor also got into the conservative *Bookman* and into the mildly socialistic *Metropolitan*. Mencken and George Jean Nathan (one of Benchley's favorite essayists) captured the editorship of the *Smart Set* in 1914. They turned that rather light periodical into a monthly repository solid with belles-lettres but enlivened by the wit and humor of its editors who often hid behind the joint pseudonym "Owen Hatteras." Upon the purchase of *Vanity Fair* by Condé Nast in 1913, Frank Crowninshield assumed its editorship and made that monthly into a market for humor as smart and as glossy as its format. *The New Yorker* had no exact predecessors, but the *Smart Set*, *Vanity Fair*, and the weekly *Life* had varying combinations of learning, taste, urbanity, and liveliness.

Bangs, Leacock, Herford, and the versifiers Carolyn Wells and Arthur Guiterman were among the most frequent contributors of humor to the established monthlies as well as to the comic weeklies *Life*, *Judge*, and *Puck*. Benchley's former co-workers on the *Lampoon*—Frederick Lewis Allen, Laurence McKinney, John Suter, and Paul Hollister—placed their work mainly in the quality monthlies. Clarence Day wrote largely for the *Metropolitan* and the *New Republic*. Toward the end of the decade, the market for the "new" humor became more and more hospitable to the work of such younger writers as Dorothy Parker.

Again, between 1910 and 1920 no single writer or small group of writers stood head and shoulders above other humorists. In contrast, by the middle 1920's, Will Rogers was the most popular crackerbox humorist of all time; and Sinclair Lewis and Ring Lardner were the best known satirists who worked in the more pretentious medium of fiction. But, although Benchley numbered his readers in the thousands rather than in the millions,[16] he had the highest reputation of any humorous writer among the readers for whom Ross was planning *The New Yorker*.[17]

As for Macy's prediction, Will Rogers was popular enough in 1919 for a publisher to risk printing some of his sayings in two books, *The Cowboy Philosopher on Prohibition* and *The Cowboy Philosopher on the Peace Conference*. Macy was less accurate in assuming that there would be only one satirist and one "voice and lingo." The American scene was too big and complex to be satirized thoroughly by any one person or even by a number of satirists developing variations on one character type and using one set of linguistic devices, as in the crackerbarrel tradition. To stretch a phrase of James Russell Lowell, the crackerbox writers could be said to have one "general tone"; but certain angry critics of the common man—notably Lardner, Lewis, Mencken, and Don Marquis—voiced their discontent in polytones that remind one only indirectly of the crackerbarrel. Although these four writers contributed to *The New Yorker*, their approach is, on the whole, distinct also from the urbane underplaying of Thurber, E. B. White, Charles Brackett, Frank Sullivan, and the other writers most commonly identified with the magazine.

As for Benchley, through dozens of pieces which he wrote before *The New Yorker* existed, he probably had as much to do with creating the "general tone" of this group as any other single writer. Thurber and White in particular looked to him for example and for criticism.[18]

IV *Apprentice and Free Lance*

The succession of jobs held by Benchley between 1912 and 1919 brought the family a living, but his important hours were spent at his desk in his spare time. From the idea and phrase notebook previously mentioned, a number of items found their way into print. Of those quoted in Nathaniel Benchley's biography (82-83), some, like "The ultimate reliance of all social schemes, etc., is on the individual," reveal the bent of his ideas; some, like "Leathery odor of room full of women with seal skins and hand bags," show the apprentice trying his hand at a line which was not to be especially his—vivid sensory description. Other items show him practicing ways of giving a humorous twist to a brief passage, or making repetition suggest a lack of ideas on the part of the speaker or narrator—a practice that became a mark of his style: "Outside, the wind sighed through the trees with a sound like the wind sighing in the trees." He was also using faulty parallelism more deftly: "I raised my hat, smiled, and backed into a tree."

Two days after depleting the bank of his last ten dollars, Benchley received his first check for a free-lance piece (forty dollars). "Hints on Writing a Book," which appeared in *Vanity Fair* (October, 1914), has certain features that he used throughout his career. Basic is the first-person singular, autobiographical narrative of an *alter ego*, or *persona*, who is a distortion by exaggeration of the author's faults and foibles. Through depiction of this narrator's misadventures, Benchley satirizes a self-confessed fault common also in many other persons—the tendency to make plans that are big or too difficult for their abilities. This fault is the symptom of another, deeper one: the belief in a false and flattering image of oneself. Possibly this belief is an underlying subject in all humor and satire.

"My idea was to create something big in fiction," says the inflated, fictitious Benchley. He has thought of writing a novel about "the oppressed working classes" which would be "Strong, you know, and uncompromising in its language, yet something you wouldn't be ashamed to put in leather and have your friends surprise you with on your bon-bon dish table." However, by the time he has his typewriter fitted into the card room, he has "given up the cause of the working classes, owing to an unpleasant altercation I had had with the man who puts in our coal." His second choice is "the present tendency toward immorality on the stage," but he abandons this idea after being bullied by a ticket seller into purchasing a bad seat at "one of the more 'frank'

ROBERT BENCHLEY

plays." Then he decides on "some quiet little story of disappointed love, with just enough psychic interest to make it unintelligible and therefore 'well worth reading.'" He gets no farther
than the title: "No Matter From What Angle You Look At It,
Alice Brookhausen Was a Girl Whom You Would Hesitate To
Invite Into Your Own Home."

This would-be author is like millions of men without literary
ambitions in having a home, a family, and the minor annoyances
resulting therefrom, including a teething baby. The caricature
of a lazy and pretentious fellow very much like anyone also
contains implications about conspicuous display of culture, overbearing tradesmen and clerks, soupy love stories, highbrow psychological fiction, wordy and sensational titles, pompous phraseology by autobiographical writers, and an affected interest in
problem novels on the part of middle-class people who distrust
the lower classes. The satire is light, but its targets are domestic,
social, and literary. Techniques include simple repetition ("The
typewriter is a vast improvement over the old-fashioned papyrusand-toothpick method of the—er, papyrus-and-toothpick period.")
and portentous triteness ("Goodness knows, it's little enough
good we can do in this world without finding fault.").

Lacking as yet in Benchley's style are consistent deftness and
unexpected, recurrent daftness. Only once does he achieve the
slippery ease that later caught readers off guard: "As I stood in
the Subway with my mouth in the velvet bow on a lady's hat…"
The zany non-sequitur is absent, and the piece in consequence
lacks the air of lunacy which eventually separated Benchley
from many other humorists who likewise caricatured themselves
as bumblers.

In the next piece which he sold—also to *Vanity Fair* (August,
1915)—Robert tackled the problem of how to write in the light
style that he was finding he could do better, and better and yet
how to avoid frivolity—that is, how not to ignore completely the
rumblings in Europe. This essay, "A Warning Note in the Matter
of Preparedness," opened with a thrust against those who would
strengthen the armed forces, but turned out to be a speech about
what's wrong with education, purportedly delivered by a pompous citizen running for School Committeeman. Parts of the
"talk" concerned this citizen's difficulties when he was a schoolboy; as a bumbler, the boy was father of the man. Benchley had

[40]

found his proper medium, the short monologue, narrative or familiar essay in which he depicted an inept little character based partly on himself and partly on the same kind of figure developed by John Kendrick Bangs, Franklin P. Adams, Simeon Strunsky, and Heywood Broun, as well as by Sinclair Lewis in his first novel, *Our Mr. Wrenn* (1914). Through the subsequent work of Benchley, Clarence Day, Jr., and other younger men, this figure was becoming a dominant type.

In the pictorial comic strips, Mr. Milquetoast and Dagwood Bumstead were, of course, to become better known Little Men than any of the types confined to the printed word. In the movies, Charles Chaplin was influential by about 1914; and, on the stage, Joe Jackson and Ed Wynn portrayed their own hilarious versions of bewildered fumblebums. If the twentieth century was the century of the common man, the 1920's and 1930's were to be, in' humor, a period stressing one particular type of common man.

While working for the New York *Tribune* Sunday magazine (1916-1917), Benchley began a series of parodies with the running title "Popular Science." Included were such articles as "Did Prehistoric Man Walk on His Head?" and "Do Jelly Fish Suffer Embarrassment?" Thus he had found another of his future lines—expressing his lifelong distrust of science by parody of its popularizers. But Robert was still too uncertain of his peculiar talents and was still trying too hard to write "serious" pieces. The editor of *Collier's* accepted three of his brief essays but warned that Benchley's writing was "too collegiate." Indeed, a forcing of effect—the besetting sin of campus humorists—marked such passages as "Then there are the transalpine relatives of the man who is entitled to a football ticket application, who lie in a comatose state of uncommunicativeness all the year, only to make themselves known in the late fall with bland suggestions of avenues of disposal for any extra seats he may be able to wheedle out of the captain of the team."[19] Even flatter than the *Collier's* pieces is a primarily informative article in *World Outlook* (October, 1916) about the development of the chewing-gum industry.

And so Benchley's own development was slow; and, even as he gradually evolved and perfected his style as a humorist, he remained unsure of whether he wanted to be one. By 1915, three years after leaving Harvard, he had such a reputation among alumni as an after-dinner monologuist that the president of his alma mater insisted on speaking before rather than after Benchley because "He knew that to follow him would be suicide."[20] But Robert wanted to be a writer, not a funnyman. Despite an offer during that year from Paul R. Reynolds, already a successful literary agent and later one of the best-known agents in the business, to handle a "funny story" if Benchley would write one, he refused to oblige.[21]

CHAPTER *3*

A Yank Who Wasn't Coming

I *Two Attitudes Toward War*

BENCHLEY'S growth as a humorist was complicated by the American entry into World War I. Benchley, twenty-five years old and a father, was draft exempt, older, and less foot-loose than John Dos Passos, Ernest Hemingway, and e. e. cummings who had already become ambulance drivers, or than F. Scott Fitzgerald, William Faulkner, and E. B. White, who trained in combat units. Moreover, Benchley's attitude toward the war and toward America's participation in it was mixed and troubled. Partly because of the death of his older brother Edmund in the Spanish-American War, Robert was an outspoken pacifist before the United States declaration of war in April, 1917. On the eve of that event, he wrote,

> Whatever comes, I don't see how our actually going into the war will be the way to settle anything—war never settles anything. I am hovering between a desire to see German Prussianism buried for the good of the future world's peace, and the feeling that if war is wrong it is wrong, and no pratings of honor can justify it.[1]

Meanwhile he had a family to feed. He clung to his job with the interventionist *Tribune;* and in March, 1917, he sent his first contribution to *Life,* despite the saber-rattling of its editors. It was rejected.[2] From January 3 to May 4, 1918, he worked as a censor for the Aircraft Board in Washington, D.C. While still working for the *Tribune,* "He saw a chance to strike a small blow for his cause" by retracing the route of Paul Revere (*not* on horseback) and asking people what they thought about America's getting involved in the war: "He was sure that the Middle-sex Yankees would be as strongly against it as he was." On the route, he became too embarrassed to go through with the plan; so he noted some local color, faked the quotes as he thought people would have responded, and wrote the story anyway. It ran as he wrote it, with no kickbacks.[3]

During this year (1918), Paul Revere's feat continued to inspire Benchley ironically. He thoroughly disliked his job as a Federal censor, and he parodied military press releases with "A Bas the Military Censor: The Ride of Paul Revere—As It Would Be Featured in Washington Today" in *Chips Off the Old Benchley* (349-53). After the war he did two more pieces about the Boston silversmith, one in which Paul saw a vision of the future that included "five million youths, cheered on by a hundred million elders with fallen arches, marching out to give their arms and legs and lives for Something To Be Determined Later" in *Pluck and Luck*. Dos Passos and Hemingway were not more bitter.

During the war, Benchley resolved, if not solved, the problem of how to write light pieces without violating his social conscience. He fired at limited targets like wartime red tape, petty bureaucracy, and spy hysteria—see "Have You a Little German Agent in Your Home"—and he worked into his articles little jabs at the ignorance, gullibility, and irrationality of the average man—the man who, Mark Sullivan said, was of unparalleled importance in this century.[4] "A Warning Note in the Matter of Preparedness" opens with "At this time, when we have suddenly become so woefully unprepared in everything pertaining to the defense of the integrity of our firesides and our national honor (whatever that may be)...." In the same piece, Benchley's *alter ego*, ostensibly discussing education, says, "Now, here is an issue which is too big for any one man to settle, which relieves me of any responsibility, and yet no possible odium can fall on me for stirring it up." A piece on the hysteria of football fans ends with a subordinate clause about how this hysteria, "when embracing a wider range, becomes what we call patriotism." A parody stressing the futile talkiness of the United States Senate—published in the politically aloof *Vanity Fair*—pays due attention to official comments on glory.[5] In Benchley's factual article on chewing-gum, the author hints at the connection between war, diplomacy, and economic self-interest: "Thus it is that Mexico and the United States are joined by ties that transcend diplomacy, and woe to

the Administration or the Opposition through whose machina-
tions the supply of chewing-gum is cut off and the bulwark of
our Democracy shattered."[6]

Occasionally Benchley's impatience with the common man and
his misleaders erupted in satire like that of the angry iconoclasts
—William Brann, Ambrose Bierce, E. W. Howe, and H. L. Mencken—men whose invective and satire were usually quite distinct
from the mellower voices of Bangs, Leacock, and Day. Benchley,
through "Vox Populi," blistered the "Average Voter" by describing his conduct on election day:

> Votes for head of ticket as recommended by his morning
> paper. Forgets what paper said about the rest of the offices so
> votes straight Republocrat ticket to save time. Finds friend's
> name again, in another party column. Votes for him too. Any-
> way, his opponent's name was Harold. Has a suspicion that he
> has spoiled his ballot, but decides that if they don't like it they
> know what they can do with it.[7]

Published shortly after the Armistice, "The Making of a Red"
narrates how a man made a speech about "Inter-Urban High-
ways" that was twisted by the government into a Bolshevist
attempt at subversion. The press attacks him, his friends desert
him, and he is driven into becoming the red-shirted toter of TNT
he has been accused of being. Thus early, Benchley joined the
war against bigotry that has been part of the tradition of white-
collar humor despite its careful aloofness and understatement.
"The Making of a Red" anticipates Thurber's parable of perse-
cution containing the ironic moral that "Anybody who you or
your wife thinks is going to overthrow the government by violence must be driven out of the country."[8] Even as Mencken
deliberately sought arrest in Boston for selling an "obscene"
magazine, Benchley would march in a demonstration for Sacco
and Vanzetti and would make a deposition against Judge Thayer.[9]

However, unlike such iconoclastic predecessors as Ambrose
Bierce, Mencken, and E. W. Howe, Benchley really believed in
the validity of democracy and of the voting process. The pre-
rogatives of the comatose citizen (in "Vox Populi") "somehow
seem sadly in need for the exercise"; he should concern himself
more, not less, with public issues. In all of their blasts at the
Great American Boob as citizen, Benchley and Thurber resemble

Bierce, Mencken, and others in their contempt for the common man's ignorance and apathy; but they do not share the belief of the iconoclasts that this condition is permanent and hopeless.

The pieces cited in the three preceding paragraphs were written mostly in the third person singular, with the author usually absent or omniscient. The bumbler speaking in the first person constituted a point of view which, at that time, Benchley could not, or at any rate did not, adapt to satirical discussion of big issues. "Doing Your Bit in the Garden"[10] is effective humor based on one of the fringe features of the war, the Victory gardens. "The Will to Suffer"[11] also illustrates Benchley's reversion to the first person in handling material less urgent than war and social injustice; and, in addition, it shows his need, at least in his capacity as author, somehow to hold two separate attitudes—one toward war and its related problems, the other toward less frightening matters. In attacking the pessimism of current poetry and fiction, the speaker commends the battle-pieces of Wilfrid Gibson because they deal with "legitimate horror" but criticizes the gloomy over-view in poems by the same writer that have nothing to do with the war. Benchley proclaims, "I am not one of the Pollyanna band, but I think that I would prefer Pollyanna to Thomas Hardy to have about the house day in and day out." Benchley carefully restrained his satire about the war and its implications, but the flimsiness of his rationalization—actually he would have loathed Miss Eleanor Porter's dogmatic little optimist —suggests guilt feelings about this self-restraint.

II A "Literary Fracture"

Benchley's uncertainties about the war illustrate what Charles Fenton has called a "literary fracture"—the disruption between the pre-war and post-war generations of writers that forms a landmark in our literary history.[12] Only a handful of the older writers, including E. A. Robinson, Robert Frost, Carl Sandburg, Edgar Lee Masters, and Theodore Dreiser bridged the generations with little change in outlook and reputation. Others in the senior generation lost the respect of the younger writers through "the extraordinary willingness of the older writers to lend their prestige and talent to the most bloodthirsty and archaic aspects of the war."[13] Henry James became a British subject; John Burroughs lectured on "Kruppism, Kaiserism, and Prussianism"; Edith Wharton threw herself into relief work in France. In various ways William Gillette, Bliss Carman, Thomas Sergeant Perry, George Edward Woodberry, Hamilton Wright Mabie, and Brander Matthews qualified for leadership in Benchley's crowd of "elders with fallen arches." So, after much soul-searching, did John Dewey who was promptly flayed for his support of America's entry into the war by Randolph Bourne, one of the few pacifists who stuck to his principles.[14]

The split among humorists between pre-war and post-war writers was not so clear, partly because humorous writers in America tended to avoid the crucial issues and to pick around on the fringes of the war for their subject matter. The guns of August, 1914, did not interrupt Ring Lardner's production of the Jack Keefe letters and the stories included in *Gullible's Travels* (1917) and *Own Your Own Home* (1919). However, Lardner's relative indifference to the war, and the public demand that the American soldier be treated kindly in print, doubtless had much to do with the ineffectiveness of his two books about Keefe's adventures as a doughboy.[15] Anti-war humor by Art Young and others sparkled in the Socialist weekly *The Masses,* but the popular crackerbox oracle Kin Hubbard made "Abe Martin" concentrate largely on home-front problems. Don Marquis isolated his patriotism in serious lyrics about "the Beast" Nietzsche and the "mighty mother" France[16] while he went on filling his column with prose satires of suffragettes and poetasters and with poems about Archy and Mehitabel. Mencken turned from humor to philology (publishing the first version of *The American Language* in 1919) rather than bring himself and his associates into trouble through his pro-German views. Edward Streeter, in the training-camp humor of *Dere Mable,* wrote one of the few pieces about major wartime activities that still finds a handful of readers. For one reason or another, most humorists, like Benchley, tended to bypass the war; and one may suspect that their reticence often concealed perplexities similar to his.

Indirectly, the war stimulated American humor in one way: it brought Franklin P. Adams, Alexander Woollcott, and Harold Ross together on the editorial staff of *Stars and Stripes,* the official newspaper of the American Expeditionary Force. Much of what Ross learned in this job of building a lively periodical was to go into his editorship of *The New Yorker,* and Woollcott was to become, off and on, one of the more prominent contributors to that magazine.

In short, the "war of democracy" silenced one or two humorists, stimulated a few, discouraged others, and caused self-distrust and division of spirit in many. Benchley, after the Armistice, was much relieved and "had a magnificent time"[17] writing "The Community Masque as a Substitute for War." In it he allowed good-natured funpoking at suburban mores to overbalance some sharper satire of mass susceptibility to war and postwar hysteria. In 1917 he had sent a piece to *Life* (a humorous weekly not to be confused with Henry Luce's magazine of the same name), and within three years after the war he joined that magazine as drama critic. Benchley's lack of antagonism toward the interventionist *Life,* plus the wide variety in the wartime careers of other practicing and future humorists, is an example of how the rupture of continuity between the prewar and post-war generations of humorists was much less clearcut, if it could be said to exist at all, than among more portentous writers.[18] The real cleavage in humor—that between the crackerbox philosophers and the university wits—owed its origin to industrialization, the urbanizing and suburbanizing of the populace, the breakdown of nineteenth-century values, and many other interrelated forces of which war was not the least but was only one.

CHAPTER 4

Editor, Columnist, Author of Books

I N 1919 the managing editor of *Collier's* helped Benchley find himself as a writer by suggesting that he do a series of pieces "with himself as the poor boob." About that time Benchley became managing editor of *Vanity Fair;* soon thereafter he was working on the "old" *Life,* and these two magazines reaped most of the benefits from the rival editor's suggestion.

I *The Anti-Organization Man*

Somewhat unfairly, Ring Lardner once referred to "correct Crowninshield dinner English,"[1] implying a stuffiness in *Vanity Fair* that Benchley, Dorothy Parker, and Robert E. Sherwood did much to alleviate during their brief stay with the magazine. Among monthlies, *Vanity Fair* and the *Smart Set* led in combining learning with liveliness. *Vanity Fair* was ancient, as American magazines went, having been founded in 1868; but it was rejuvenated after Condé Nast, the wealthy owner of *Vogue,* bought it and hired Frank Crowninshield as editor in 1913. Crowninshield turned it into a sophisticated, satirical review of literature, the arts, theater, and society. He steered clear of politics and practiced decorum in the treatment of sex and of language.

The views of John Jay Chapman, as stated during the managing editorship of Benchley under Crowninshield, are consistent with the policy of the magazine: "The educated classes are, at every epoch, the people who conserve any language: the rest adopt it ... it is by our literacy we stand."[2] Concerning sex, Crowninshield objected to a paragraph about the mating of newts in Benchley's "The Social Life of the Newt," although Nathaniel Benchley points out justly that no newt could have distinguished this passage from an account of a rare-book auction.[3]

On the other hand, the magazine was venturesome in its hospitality to European authors previously little known in the United States; and it was outdone in this respect by only the *Smart Set*. Arthur Schnitzler, Paul Geraldy, Colette, André Maurois, Ferenc Molnar, and Paul Morand were among the younger Europeans who benefited from this hospitality during and shortly after Benchley's editorship. Their work appeared alongside humor by the managing editor, by Miss Parker, and by G. K. Chesterton, P. G. Wodehouse, A. A. Milne, A. H. Folwell, George Chappell, Leacock, Broun, Charles Brackett, Frederick Lewis Allen, and Paul Hollister. Young illustrators who contributed regularly included Rea Irvin, Gluyas Williams, Al Frueh, Anne Harriet Fish, and Rollin Kirby.

These writers had to meet the standard implied in Benchley's profile of Crowninshield written for the *Bookman*, another highbrow publication:

> He believes that the hope of a revival of Good Taste lies in those men and women who are college graduates, have some money, who know porcelains, and Verlaine, and Italian art, who love Grolier bindings, Spanish brocades, and French literature, and who do not consider it high-brow to be able to understand other languages than American—and baseball. . . . He makes up in some degree for this adherence to the old form by his willingness for any writer who writes entertainingly, to say practically anything he wants to say in "Vanity Fair"—so long as he says it in evening clothes.[4]

With this policy, "Crownie" offered competition to the self-styled "Aristocrat of Magazines"—the *Smart Set*. A few details about the careers of writers for *Vanity Fair* during Benchley's tenure show how the older and newer strains of genteel humor blended during the post-war, pre-*New Yorker* years. Chesterton, Milne, and Wodehouse were British writers in the earlier *Punch* tradition of unobtrusive learning and urbane high-jinks. Folwell had been an editor of *Puck*, and Chappell a leading contributor to *Life*, another of the older comic weeklies. Benchley, Allen, Hollister, and Sherwood had cut their stylistic teeth working on the *Lampoon*. Folwell, Broun, and Benchley had been associated in newspaper work. Brackett, Wilson (Princeton, 1916), and Miss Parker would contribute later to *The New Yorker* along with most of these other writers; and Brackett would be replaced as drama critic on that magazine by Benchley.

Now that *Vanity Fair* paid him a salary for writing pretty much as he liked, Benchley seemed well launched as a humorist. Usually he did two pieces a month, one of which appeared under his own name and the other under the pseudonym "Brighton Perry." Some of his *Vanity Fair* pieces were parodies without authorial comment, but most featured the mishaps of a character who resembled Thurber's yet nonexistent Walter Mitty, except that no domineering wife was included among his troubles (Thurber once wrote that the typical writer of "light pieces" worries about whether "a piece he has been working on for two long days was done much better and probably more quickly by Robert Benchley in 1924."[5] In 1919, Robert's little man tried to improve his memory through word-association, later one of Thurber's favorite exercises. Benchley's bumbler had met a Mr. Conchman and promptly forgotten the man's name:

> The man's beard is blonde and sparse. It might be said (if one were very anxious to say it) that it resembles ensilage. Ensilage is found in a *silo*, and *silo*, you will remember, is one of the list of sixty mystic words I memorized this morning. It was, in fact, fourth in the list. Next to it came *what-not*. Now, let us review the objects that are usually found on a what-not. There may be a hand-painted china shepardess [sic], a mother-of-pearl papercutter bearing a picture of a ferris-wheel and the legend "Greetings from the Centenary," a sweet-grass miniature demijohn, a conch-shell—that's it—a *conch-shell*, and the man's name is Conchman![6]

Much of Robert's humor had an anti-organization slant that was only a slight exaggeration of his personal relations with governmental machinery and business bureaucracies. Benchley, Sherwood, and Dorothy Parker made their stay at *Vanity Fair* brisk and brief with gay rebellion against office routine and managerial arrogance. Something of the collegiate spirit flashed when Benchley let Sherwood (who, like himself, had supervised a parody issue of the *Lampoon*) write half of the column, "What the Well-Dressed Man Will Wear," the regular columnist having gone on vacation. "Several advertisers kicked up a ruckus,"[7] but Nast and Crowninshield were also away, and their complaints to Benchley got nowhere. Neither did Nast's office manager when he threatened to discharge any employee who disclosed the amount of his salary. Benchley wrote a scathing memo of protest, and he and his two associates went around for awhile with signs hung on their necks, on which were written the amounts of their stipends. Such antics worsened the relations between the trio and Nast; the firing of Dorothy Parker, after cries of pain over her drama reviews had come to Nast from actress Billie Burke and three leading producers, merely broke the tension.[8] For the second time Benchley quit an admittedly insecure job because of injustice done to a friend.

II "Books and Other Things"

By this time Benchley must have been in some demand as a columnist. He set out to do some free-lance writing, working in an office he shared with Dorothy Parker—an office so small that, as he said later, "one cubic foot less of space and it would have constituted adultery."[9] Within a month of leaving *Vanity Fair*, he signed with Pulitzer's New York *World* to do a thrice-weekly department, "Books and Other Things," at one hundred dollars a week, the same salary with which he had started as a managing editor.

Although the point of departure for each day's column was supposed to be the book, or books, that he was reviewing, Benchley was allowed to branch out a good deal from straight reviews. By playing the role of bumbler-as-book-reviewer, he often supplied a humorous if not logical justification for exercising his freedom and, at the same time, kept subtly reminding his readers not to expect mere book reviews from his department. In his first column he claimed that it had taken him seventeen months to read H. G. Wells' *Joan and Peter*, and

"Either I have got to speed up, or else the whole established system and convention of book reviewing has got to be upset to make room for what I am going to do. On the whole, I think that the latter way would be simpler, because I am quite sure that I can't read any faster."[10]

Often he deviated into parody of the volume ostensibly under review, or into humorous treatment of a subject only touched upon in that volume. He honored *Main Street* with a parody, and used Albert Bigelow Paine's *Moments with Mark Twain* and Franklin P. Adams' *Something Else Again* as points of departure for a discussion of dialect humor versus humor in correct English—resolved in favor of the latter.[11]

Behind Robert's self-belittlement sat a perceptive critic who approved of the trend toward stark realism in the novels of that important year—up to a point. During 1920 he praised *Main Street*,[12] Sherwood Anderson's *Poor White* (although he thought it "foggy" and "an anti-climax" in comparison with Lewis' novel[13]), Zona Gale's *Miss Lulu Bett*,[14] and Floyd Dell's *Mooncalf*. His second thoughts on Lewis, however, included the parody in which he satirized Lewis' "flair for minutia";[15] and, in reviewing *Mooncalf*, he warned that he had had enough of realistic novels on smalltown life in the Midwest.[16] Here, as elsewhere, he was a little in the forefront of literary trends while hanging suspiciously back from the *avant garde*. He could see the limitations of Lewis, but he was extremely severe toward James Joyce and Faulkner.[17]

III *"Life" and the Theater*

No matter how much money Benchley made, he was always reaching into his pockets and finding them empty; perhaps this was why he sometimes took on so many jobs at once. In addition to "Books" he had, in April of 1920, received his dream job —drama critic on *Life;* and in 1921 he began a syndicated weekly news column for David Lawrence. His bosses on the *World* objected to Benchley's writing for other newspapers, and the "Books" column was dropped; he found the current-events column so uncongenial that he let it die after six months.[18] Down to one job again, he was soon placing free-lance work regularly with *Life* and other periodicals.

Benchley ran the drama department of *Life* from 1921 to 1929, during nearly all of the so-called roaring 1920's. Under the presidency of Charles Dana Gibson and the editorship of E. S. Martin, *Life* refused to roar but confined itself to chuckles and to well-bred growls. The humorous tone of the magazine was dampened by plenty of serious moralizing, and this policy was evidently not entirely suited to the times. *Life* reached its peak of circulation (about 250,000) the year before Benchley joined the magazine; thereafter it gradually declined.

One number in the early 1920's (an issue unusual only because it was the one in which Benchley first took over the theater section: April 29, 1920) included a large amount of poetry, more than half of which was serious; two pages of rather stodgy editorials; a long, earnest discussion of a fund-raising project for the support of war orphans; and an equally serious discussion of spiritualism. The only verses that really sparkled were those by Oliver Herford; the only humorous prose pieces longer than about a hundred and fifty words were an essay on traffic regulation by Henry William Hanneman and an anonymous parody of George H. Lorimer's *Letters of a Self-Made Merchant to His Son.* Most of the humor in this issue was found in anonymous fillers of one hundred words or less (many of them probably done by the managing editor, Thomas L. Masson) and in the drawings, which were livelier than the prose. In the next few issues the high points in humor were just as infrequent and were supplied by Agnes Repplier, Grant M. Overton, "Baron Ireland" (Nate Saulsbury), and Robert E. Sherwood. The illustrators were Rea Irvin, Gluyas Williams, Charles Dana Gibson, Percy Crosby, H. T. Webster, and Russ Westover.

Once again, the careers of these men show how old ways in humor mixed with the new. Gibson had created the robust but chaste "Gibson girl" in the 1890's. Irvin became a mainstay of *The New Yorker;* Williams illustrated Benchley's books; and Crosby, Webster, and Westover created "Skippy," "The Timid Soul," and "Tillie the Toiler," respectively, for other periodicals. Some of the new blood needed by the magazine came also from Dorothy Parker, Marc Connelly, and George S. Kaufman.

One of Benchley's early effects on the magazine was evident in a 'Burlesque Number" (September 8, 1921), in which Connelly and others collaborated in parodying some of *Life's* contemporaries, including the *Saturday Evening Post,* the *New Republic,* and *Popular Mechanics.* The issue was inspired by Benchley's parody of *Life* in the *Lampoon;*[19] every copy printed was sold, and it was reprinted twice in subsequent years.

Whether these transfusions would have sustained *Life* had not *The New Yorker* risen as a competitor, no one can now say. Thurber reminisced that, by 1928, the chief reason people bought

Life was Benchley.[20] Benchley finished moving over to *The New Yorker* by 1929, and he was already writing "The Wayward Press" for it. Most of the other young contributors to *Life* gradually transferred their energies to Ross's magazine at about that time or shortly thereafter.[21] If we count only his work for *Life*, the *Bookman*, and *The New Yorker*, Benchley ground out drama criticism for seventeen consecutive seasons. Even a brief glance at this large body of material sharpens the outlines of his white-collared Little Man as Wise Fool.[22] Benchley's basic approach to reviewing plays—like all his writing, the reverse of dispassionate—was to depict himself as a bumbling but basically sensible fellow who happened to be sizing up plays instead of selling suits or running an office. Any difference between him and the rest of the theater-going public (Benchley pretended) arose merely from his having more time and more incentive to see and to think about plays. He claimed to know nothing about the history of the drama or about the techniques of playwriting: "I always know that a play is clumsily written if I can detect passages in it that I myself might have done."[23]

He wrote for the playgoer who has taste but who, primarily out for an evening of pleasure, does not ordinarily like to have *avant-garde* experiments tried on him. Concerning Shaw's *The Apple Cart* and the pantomimes of Mei Lan-fang, Benchley asked, "Why *need* we be bored? Why should we have to make allowances for *anything* when we go for entertainment?"[24] On the other hand, if it gripped the audience, Benchley had a place for a play in his credo regardless of how highbrow or lowbrow it might be. *The Bat* was "full of hokum, tricks, and much unnecessary lying. . . . But it certainly is a grand show!"[25] Of *Mourning Becomes Electra* he said that O'Neill "gives us nothing to think about (unless we are just beginning to think), but he does thrill the bejeezus out of us, just as his father used to do, and that is what we go to the theatre for."[26] Benchley made shrewd and mainly favorable estimates of such pretentious experiments as George Bernard Shaw's *Heartbreak House* and *St. Joan*, George Büchner's *Wozzeck*, Anton Chekhov's *The Cherry Orchard*, T. S. Eliot's *Murder in the Cathedral*, the Russian ballet, and of boffola artists Frank Tinney, Ed Wynn, and Joe Penner.

The character types in Benchley's humor may be divided

roughly into the bumblers and the boobs, and he makes the same division, explicitly, in regard to theater audiences. The bumblers are decent if disturbed—basically "nice guys"—but the boobs are crass and insensitive, differing from most of Ring Lardner's chiefly in that they use better English. Just as Benchley's evaluation of *Mourning Becomes Electra* is addressed to the ideal middlebrow playgoer, so are his criticisms of J. M. Barrie's *Mary Rose*:

> And then there are those sentimental, childish, slightly queer people who will sit through the three acts and never notice that the meaning is hazy, or the situations strained, or that Ruth Chatterton is not the best possible actress to play the part. Most of the time they won't be able to see the stage at all because of a slight blurring of their vision.... To this third class I must admit that I belong.[27]

Benchley's ideal playgoer responds to thrills and to sentimentality, but retains his critical faculty. Unfortunately, this playgoer is rare. Benchley sarcastically defined the taste of the majority:

> It has been found by research that any American audience will applaud spontaneously at the sight of—
> 1. A back-drop showing tiny vehicles with electric lights moving across the landscape, or windows in which the lights go on as night falls.
> 2. A musical ensemble in which the entire company raises its arms and wiggles its fingers.
> 3. Large crystal chandeliers.
> 4. A musical number in which the man exits driving the girl with a pair of ribbon reins.
> 5. Any reference to America as "God's country."
> 6. The red spotlight thrown on anything at all.
> 7. A song-ending in which the last three notes involve a tenor.[28]

Benchley lists ten more tasteless but much-applauded props or situations. He also breathed fire at "the coughers, the crooners, the nine o'clock arrivals," and at those women who giggle at swear words and sexual allusions and who generally titter at the wrong things. Once he offered to pay for the seats of two gigglers if they would leave the theater.[29]

It was partly his own reticence about sex and partly the child-ish reactions of the booboisie that made Benchley wonder if "the whole institution of Sex has been a mistake."[30] According to Nathaniel, he never got over his embarrassment at jokes about sex, and he once stormed from a dirty show and personally bawled out the producer. Toward the end of the 1920's he announced that "Sex, as a theatrical property, is as tiresome as the Old Mortgage, and that I don't want to hear it mentioned ever again."[31] However, it was sex and dirt for its own sake that he disliked, especially if presented with a snigger.

Of *Lysistrata* he said, "It is frankly and openly a comedy of sex, and it seems to me, by its frankness and openness, quite clean."[32] He approved of the profanity of *What Price Glory?*, by Maxwell Anderson and Laurence Stallings, as "true-talk," and he rejected the proposition that plays be censored with this question: "Who is going to do the censoring?"[33] The only proper censor, he hinted, was the thoughtful playgoer—himself, for instance—operating through reviews and through the box office without benefit of legal power. And the only proper criterion was the play as a play. It was all very well to award the Pulitzer Prize to *Miss Lulu Bett* for " raising the standard of good morals, good taste and good manners'," but "How about a prize some day for the best piece of dramatic writing?"[34]

How many readers of *Life* helped to give Anne Nichols' *Abie's Irish Rose* a record run despite Benchley's strictures is impossible to say, but his reviews in general earned him respect among theater people. A poll of actors, taken in 1927, on which critics were the most "discriminating" and "stimulating," rated Benchley second to Alexander Woollcott by two votes. Benchley's role as the thoughtful middlebrow was, however, in part a carryover from his predecessor, James Metcalfe, an em-ployee of *Life* since its founding, who had often proclaimed the same affinity for taste without fastidiousness. When Benchley carried his own attitudes unchanged to *The New Yorker*, he wove one more thread in the continuity of earlier, genteel essay-writing with the smarter, tougher metropolitanism of the 1920's and 1930's.

IV *Benchley's Books*

The humor on which Benchley's reputation as a writer rests

is largely contained in the six hundred-odd essays, articles, sketches, narratives, and dialogues originally done for periodicals and somewhat unsystematically republished in ten books between 1921 and 1938. Although he collected material for a full-length historical play about the Queen Anne period,[35] he published no single masterpieces of scope and depth enough to warrant sustained analysis. Rather, his impact is in the total effect of a large number of short pieces, whether read in Benchley's first ten books or in the four anthologies of material reprinted from them. Therefore, instead of being a piece-by-piece discussion of separate contributions, our next chapter will discuss the themes and ideas which crop up most frequently in Benchley's writing as a whole.

However, a brief look, volume by volume, of some of Benchley's books may help give an overview of his writing career. *Of All Things!* (1921) is made up largely of material which Benchley wrote for *Vanity Fair* and *Life,* although he drew on *Collier's* and *Motor Print* for several selections and on the old Sunday *Magazine* of the New York *Tribune for* "Call for Mr. Kenworthy!" The most effective touches of what Dorothy Parker recalled as the "old madness"—not so old then—of Benchley are his irrelevant dedication of the book to Henry Bessemer for having invented the steel converter and his acknowledgment of various magazines for permission to reprint this material: "As a matter of fact, permission was never asked, but they probably won't mind anyway." Three parodies of well-known magazines are placed together as "Tabloid Editions," and in *Love Conquers All* (1922), his second volume, twenty-eight selections from his book column in the New York *World* are grouped under "Literary Department"; otherwise no scheme for arrangement of the pieces in these first two volumes is discernible. In fact, many of the selections in the second book were written before some of those in the first.

Three years passed after the publication of *Love Conquers All* before *The Early Worm,* his third collection, appeared; but this volume and subsequent collections do not differ greatly from the first two in content or in quality. By the time Benchley's second book was assembled, he had fully developed his style and had hit a plateau of quality. "The Social Life of the Newt," one of his most hilarious pieces, leads off his first collection; and

"The Treasurer's Report" winds up his sixth (although composed several years earlier). One of his best parodies, "Family Life in America," is in his second book, and another, "Love Among the Thinkers," strengthens *From Bed to Worse*, his eighth compilation. The pieces in his last two original collections, *My Ten Years in a Quandary* and *After 1903—What?*, tend to be shorter than those in the previous books, possibly because many of them were culled from the column of chit-chat he was grinding out three times a week for King Features Syndicate during 1933-1936. By the time he dropped the King column, writing had become a chore; but some of his best quips and paragraphs pepper these two volumes.

Benchley announced in 1943 that he was through writing. Few humorists, he felt, remained funny much beyond the age of fifty; and, for whatever the fact is worth, Robert was forty-nine when his last original collection appeared in 1938. Besides, Hollywood was claiming more of his time. Like his friends Dorothy Parker and Donald Ogden Stewart, and like many other talented writers, Benchley rose as a movie-maker while dying as a writer.

CHAPTER 5

The Uncommon Common Man
as Theme and Idea

EITHER directly or through satire, Benchley aired many opinions about the American common man, the family, suburbia, business, politics, science, nature, travel, literature, the fine arts, and the fine art of humor itself. Most of these opinions came from a bumbler who might be a Dagwood in his disorganized approach to home and business routines but was no Milquetoast in his defense of reason and sanity. Benchley's bumbler did not wholly possess these qualities, but he knew what they were—and he also knew how loose was his grip on them. These two items of knowledge were the beginnings of his wisdom.

I *Normal Neurotic versus Mass-Man*

In "Books and Other Things," Benchley once named the few authors whom he would enjoy on any subject they cared to write about.[1] The only modern Americans who qualified were columnists Simeon Strunsky, Frank Moore Colby, E. S. Martin, George Jean Nathan, and Heywood Broun. Just below on the list of favorites were George Ade and Will Rogers (the only crackerbox oracles Benchley cared for), Stephen Leacock, Ring Lardner, and, later, S. J. Perelman.[2]

All of these writers, plus Don Marquis and H. L. Mencken, both of whom Benchley read with qualified approval, made important use of contrasts between the man with common-sense and integrity and the mindless mass of average slobs or boobs. This man of good sense might be a wise-cracking cowboy, an angry conservative, a Mittymousy clerk, or a meditative professor. In larger works outside the pale of Benchley's favorites, he might be a prosperous lawyer like Seneca Doane in Lewis' *Babbitt*, a talkative sewing-machine agent like V. K. Ratliff in Faulkner's Snopes trilogy, or a quizzical, detached bond-salesman like Fitzgerald's Nick Carraway. In any case the basic contrasts of integrity versus expediency and of thought versus unthought are there, core-ingredients of American literature.

Bernard DeVoto and Walter Blair have claimed that Benchley, Thurber, and Perelman are "Perfect Neurotics" who differ from the nineteenth-century literary comedians in that such humorists as Mark Twain and Artemus Ward made a distinction between unsound, sometimes quite mad characters and the sane, clear-thinking authors. A modern humorist, such as Benchley, stresses the resemblances of his character to the author. Certainly Blair's profile of Benchley's favorite archetype fits Robert himself with little need for alteration:

> The character he [Benchley] pretends to be time after time is prevented from doing a number of harmless things he would like to do—leave a party when he wants to, smoke a cigarette, wear a white suit, waltz, make faces, pick flowers, and so on *ad infinitum*. The frustrations have given this character, so the collected pieces show, a mess of phobias and complexes which he shows at work on innumerable occasions. A reader is not surprised to find this assumed character ticking off one after another the symptoms of dementia praecox and finding that he has all of them.[3]

But neither Benchley nor his narrator does have dementia praecox, and the Little Man's fussing about his mental state is part of the author's technique for satirizing psychoanalysis, bad party manners, and many other things. Sometimes that technique includes direct cirticism from the narrator, who at such times is saner than the people or institutions he criticizes.

In addition, this little man is perpetually searching for his identity, his "true" self—a fitting and proper quest for any thoughtful modern man, and one that has been important in American literature from Thoreau, that well-known odd-ball at Walden Pond, to Holden Caulfield, the somewhat less appealing psychoneurotic who flunked out of Pennsy Prep. With more composure than Dick Diver in F. Scott Fitzgerald's *Tender Is the Night,* Benchley's little man decides that his inability to "toddle along" when the party's over is a sign of a general breakup of personality in which "The next step is, I am afraid, that I won't be able to find myself at all."[4] Yet he hangs on to himself in a way that Diver does not.

The quest for identity is also reflected in the little man's role-playing; he continually builds up false and flattering images of himself, and fails to live up to them. Thus, in "Take the Witness" from *My Ten Years in a Quandary,* the narrator dreams of how brilliantly he would answer his crossquestioners were he on the stand. But he knows that in an actual situation he would probably be asked the wrong questions and would give the wrong answers.

Benchley's comic figure does not throb with *Sturm und Drang* like Thomas Wolfe's Eugene Gant, nor die of the quest for self-hood like Robert Mayo in O'Neill's *Beyond the Horizon.* As J. Bryan III has said, "Romeo breaks his heart; Benchley breaks his shoelace."[5] But more serious situations rarely force Benchley's man into what Freud called "that despairing attempt at revolt— psychosis." This man views his own attempts at revolt with self-satirical detachment rather than with despair. If one type of neurosis is, as Karen Horney maintains, a detachment in which one refuses to take oneself seriously, Benchley's man is neurotic. In this sense, so are most people during some of their "rational" moments—including the earlier comedians whom Blair and DeVoto cited as sound in contrast to the fictitious types they had created.

Benchley's persona is indeed "neurotic" in being "different"— in standing as a sharp contrast to the majority of his country-men who are the equivalents of Lardner's middle-class louts and Mencken's booboisie. "How to Watch Football" (from *Pluck and Luck*) includes ironic comments by the harassed narrator about those fans who block the view and who attend to their flasks rather than to the game. These mass-men (as Ortega y Gasset called their breed in another connection) are in such a majority that all the half-way sane and considerate fan can do is to leave and to read about the game in the newspapers. Benchley was too kind to make invective a major weapon as had Mencken, but in "Whoa!" (from *Pluck and Luck*), in some of his criticisms of theater audiences, and in a few other pieces,

Robert showed that he too could pour vinegar on the heads of the "timorous, sniveling, poltroonish, ignominious mob of serfs and goosesteppers"—as Mencken had called the American people. The prospectus for the "Burlesque Number" of *Life* included, "I am the Spirit of American Magazines, dedicated to the proposition that all men are created equally stupid. And the worst of it is, I am right."[6]

II   *The Little Man at Home*

Most of the crackerbox philosophers were without sex or family and thereby stood a little apart from, although basically within, society. Abe Martin's backdrop was only the town pump and the country store; Mr. Dooley was a wistful old bachelor; Scattergood Baines (a creation of Clarence Budington Kelland) was married but ancient, and his wife was a nonentity. An exception, Will Rogers, occasionally brought his family into the picture of the cowboy-philosopher as normal citizen. In the era of Freud, flaming youth, and "companionate marriage" the targets were tempting; but Ring Lardner, Clarence Day, Jr., Heywood Broun, and Benchley were among the many humorists outside the crackerbarrel tradition who preferred to deal with sex briefly, indirectly, and decorously. For example, their characters are less monastic than the crackerbarrel philosophers but more Victorian than the husbands and wives of Thurber and Dorothy Parker: they have little sex life but are permitted by their authors to have wives and families.

The wife of Benchley's little man is a shadow, but their children! A new father when he first began to score in the magazines, Benchley stuck many pins into the sentimentalists' image of the child, an image embodied in Dickens' Little Nell and in Harriet Beecher Stowe's Little Eva, and nurtured by "progressive" educationalists and psychologists. "Childhood, as it comes fresh from the hands of God, is not corrupt, but illustrates the survival of the most consummate thing in the world. . . . Nothing else is so worthy of love and reverence, and service as the body and soul of the growing child," wrote psychologist G. Stanley Hall in 1901.[7] Benchley dedicated *Pluck and Luck* "To Nat, who helped his papa write the story on page 6 by having to go to the bath-room only seven times en route." In the New York

World, twenty-nine years before William March published *The Bad Seed,* Benchley reviewed a book about "a child after my own heart. He hated everybody." Having encountered an "oozy" narrative by the creator of Little Lord Fauntleroy about how a little girl reforms the crook who ransacked her home, Benchley wrote "Editha's Christmas Burglar," in which the child's attempts at such a reform get her slapped and tied up.[8]

Benchley was not mocking the family as an institution; he was merely needling its exploiters and sentimentalizers. He agreed with a female critic of fairy tales that gruesome narratives should be amended, but he wished that this woman wouldn't draw on *Pollyanna* by calling the new story-telling the "glad game." Beginning with an editorial in the *Lampoon,*[9] Benchley probably wrote more about Christmas than any other American humorist, and his main concern was with abuses of the Christmas spirit. In "Christmas Afternoon, Done in the Manner, if Not the Spirit, of Dickens" (*Of All Things!* [143-44]), the children are little beasts, but the Christmas spirit is impugned no more than it was by Dickens. In their personal lives, Robert and Gertrude Benchley read *A Christmas Carol* aloud every Christmas Eve for years; according to Robert's diary, they cried "not at the sad parts, but at the parts that are so glad that they shut off your wind."[10]

In debunking the child-cult, Benchley was part of a trend involving much more than the child. Henry F. May feels that American "innocence"—the naïve nineteenth-century faith in absolute truths, in progress, and in moralistic literature—began to deteriorate most rapidly and obviously between 1912 and 1917. The debunking of the child as an image of innocence and purity was surely a part of this deterioration. At the turn of the century, Stephen Crane was one of the few who dared stick out his tongue at "The Angel Child," in *Whilomville Stories;* in 1914 Booth Tarkington's *Penrod* verged on irreverence; and after World War I, Heywood Broun and F. Scott Fitzgerald (in "The Baby Party") were among those who tried to bury the child-icon. Even Thurber dealt the type a few slaps in his few pieces in which children appear.[11] Benchley may or may not have read Freud on infantile sexuality, but psychoanalysts and humorists, despite their opposition in other matters, were trying to bring to an end the innocent belief in childish innocence.

III *Nature in the Suburbs*

In *The American Humorist* I have discussed the Little Man as suburbanite, and outlined this man's relationship to the world of nature over his head and in his back yard.[12] Briefly, Benchley's narrator fumbles around the furnace and the garden, and shows a white-collar commuter's distrust for neighborhood workmen and tradesmen; but also, as in 'The Community Masque," he feels a contrast between himself and the boobs of his own "set" who bicker while he ironically looks on. In the battle with nature he is purely the comic butt; nature, according to Frank Sullivan, "had him stopped cold."[13] Sharing none of the desire of Don Marquis and E. B. White for man to recapture his lost affinity with nature, Benchley announced that "Nature can go her way and I'll go mine, just as we have gone up till now." Some terns once attacked him on the beach—probably because he spoofed the conservation movement in "Justice for Mussels" (*Pluck and Luck*) and his persona struggled unsuccessfully with soil, sun, snow, flowers, and pigeons.[14]

Many of his numerous pieces about nature were parodies of those writers and lecturers whom John Burroughs earlier had called "nature-fakers." Benchley attacked such pseudo-scientific popularizers in "Hail, Vernal Equinox," from *Of All Things!* and in passages like the following from *The Early Worm!*:

> You see, Mother Nature takes no chances. She used to, but she learned her lesson. And that is a lesson that all of you must learn as well. It is called Old Mother Nature's Lesson, and begins on page 145.
> Now, these eggs have not always been like this. That stands to reason. They once had something to do with a hen or they wouldn't be called hen's eggs. If they are called duck's eggs, that means that they had something to do with a duck. Who can tell me what it means if they are called "ostrich's egg? . . . That's right.
> But the egg is not the only thing that had something to do with a hen. Who knows what else there was? . . . That's right.[15]

One reason Benchley wrote much parody of this sort was that the popularizers were so vulnerable. The following excerpt from a radio script prepared in 1923 almost parodies itself, although the author, "Uncle Ed," was apparently trying to be serious:

Boys, don't run ahead that way. You will get lost from the party. Come back now, we are going through the woods. I will have to push a way through these high weeds. There is a path in the woods. Just follow me and we will find it. Some of you boys make a noise like a nut. Maybe we can scare up a squirrel. There is one. Listen. That is a gray squirrel. No, he doesn't make that noise with his tail. He just jerks his tail every time he makes it. Listen to him scolding. A gray squirrel can scold like everything.

Watch out. Here is some poison ivy. See that vine with the three shiny green leaves. It is on both sides of the path. So hold up your arms and hands.

No, you boys can not have that gray thing that looks like a football hanging in the tree. That is a hornet's nest. Here, big boy, don't throw stones at it. Now, you have done it. You hit their nest, and they are after us. Duck, everybody. Lie flat on the ground. Hear them flying over our heads? We will wait a minute. I guess it is safe for us to go on, but don't try that stunt again.[16]

Such effusions as this one must have stimulated Benchley almost as much as the lectures he had heard at Harvard.

IV *The Little Man versus Babbitt*

"I am known as a bad business man," Benchley admitted; and, for once, the narrator spoke accurately of his author. The mere sight of a contract or other legal document almost sent Robert into a trance, and his personal and household finances were nearly as chaotic as he suggests in "Turning Over a New Ledger Leaf," wherein the Little Man defends an inability to add and subtract with, "Who wants to be a man like that? What fun does he get out of life?"[17]

That this defense was an exaggeration of the author's views in degree rather than in kind is suggested by Benchley's worry over his inability to worry. "Damn it! I *try* to worry, and I can't," he declared.[18] Nathaniel Benchley says that "His theory was that money was intended to be spent"; after 1929 this theory put him in a position to thumb his nose at businessmen and financiers who had jeered at the impracticality of writers: "Those of us who have nothing but fripperies to show for our money have had a good laugh. At least we've got the fripperies."[19]

Perhaps the stretches as editor of a house organ and as an advertising copywriter also contributed to Benchley's delight in blowing up the myth of business "efficiency." Before Babbitt had been created, Benchley wrote as a Babbitt in "From Nine to Five" and showed "How We Make Our Business Lose $100,-000 a Year" by fumbling away the day in dictating incoherent, trivial memos, spending two hours over lunch with salesmen, and swapping jargon with other executives in a futile conference (the term "idea meeting" hadn't yet been invented). In "One Minute, Please!"[20] the Little Man as writer, "with nothing to do but finish an article which was due the day before," makes bold both to suggest that executives' misuse of the telephone is "responsible for more business inefficiency than any other agency except laudanum" and to stress their discourtesy in making one wait and in cutting off answers. The qualities that make business-men white-collar clods also make them poor executives.

In "The Treasurer's Report" the executive is just as incompe-tent at spare-time community service as in his job. One laughs mainly at the speaker's confusion, but the rest of the group is equally inept. And yet, as Benchley says with heavy irony at the end of "One Minute, Please!," "We practical businessmen have so little sympathy with a visionary, impractical arrangement like this League of Nations."

Thus did Benchley's social conscience flash out—a conscience rarely silent for long. To the tradition of Yankee reform exem-plified by Harriet Beecher Stowe, Wendell Phillips, and Edward Bellamy belonged Robert's Abolitionist grandfather, his Prohi-bitionist mother, and the "light" humorist himself. Bookish though he was, he continually involved himself with the social and political problems of the time: at Cambridge and in New York City he worked in settlement houses (the boys in Sidney Kingsley's *Dead End* reminded him of his charges in New York), and had given further time to the Urban League's attempts to improve living conditions in Harlem. He described himself as a "confused liberal." He registered Republican and often voted Democratic; supported Prohibition until the Volstead Act began to hurt, then doggedly learned to drink; distrusted the working-man and sympathized with striking waiters; was a "passionate pacifist" and supported the League of Nations.[21]

The reader may judge for himself whether Benchley was con-

fused or not, but of his courage and zeal there was no doubt.
He resigned from two jobs, and he did not mind denouncing
hoodlums to their faces.[22] Nor was there any confusion about
Benchley's attitudes toward freedom of speech, the struggle for
Negro rights, and the moral apathy of the American people.

V Political Gadflies of the 1920's

Benchley's friend Frederick Lewis Allen characterized the
1920's as the "Indian Summer" of complacent capitalism. The
autumn drowse of the relatively prosperous American middle
class was disturbed by the buzzing of a number of gadflies, of
whom Mencken was the loudest but Benchley not the least.[23]
In *Public Opinion* (1922), Walter Lippmann set forth the difficulties of communicating information on complex issues to the
man in the street; but in 1921 Benchley had presented a political
column as such a man might have written it. The piece was a
mish-mash of misinformation about the League of Nations, the
national budget, and tax problems. History as understood by
this average man included:

> This [the "funny old Greco-Turkish War"] put Napoleon III
> in a nasty position. If he turned one way, he ran full force into
> the Scylla of universal suffrage, if he turned the other he found
> himself face to face with the Pythias of revolution. Of the two,
> he chose celibacy. And the whole history of Europe was altered
> at one stroke.
>
> This brings us up to the League of Nations and its accomplish-
> ments at Lucerne—or was it Geneva?[24]

Two essays in *Love Conquers All* (1922), "The Tariff Un-
masked" and "How to Understand International Finance," likewise satirized the average man's ignorance and indifference.

The Smith-Hoover campaign of 1928 brought several gadflies
together in an angry cluster. Robert E. Sherwood, then managing editor of *Life*, organized the "Anti-Bunk" party, which
nominated Will Rogers for President. Will announced, "I chews
to run," and he campaigned through a series of articles to which
Benchley provided a counterpoint with "A Short History of
American Politics" and other satires blasting both the politicians
and the public. In a radio broadcast, Benchley chaired a meeting

of "President Will Rogers' Cabinet," members of which also included comedians Eddie Cantor, Bert Kalmar, and Harry Ruby. Other speakers in the same series of broadcasts (sponsored by *Life* and the Kolster Radio Corporation) were Amelia Earhart, Walter Winchell, songwriter Gene Buck, and actors Thomas Meighan, Leon Errol, and Raymond Hitchcock. Political satire of mass-man and of his misleaders made strange bedfellows of the "Intelligent Minority" (as Rogers characterized the Anti-Bunks).[25]

V *"Liberty and License"*

In Benchley's books after 1930 one finds less about public affairs,[26] not so much because the Great Depression aroused people from their apathy as because Benchley, after 1927, put much of what he had to say about public events into "The Wayward Press" department for *The New Yorker*. Writing under the subversive pseudonym "Guy Fawkes," he tried consciously to avoid political partiality. Thus, for example, he disavowed any concern with the merits or demerits of Franklin D. Roosevelt's plan to "pack" the Supreme Court, commenting merely that the editorial campaign against it may have reached a saturation point too early. Throughout the Depression he castigated specific periodicals without regard to their affiliation; and because the mass-circulation media were largely conservative, Benchley may have seemed more of a New Dealer than he actually was. Benchley's view of the readership, however, did not change from what it had been in 1928. Hinting that various newspapers tried to help Alf Landon to the presidency in 1936 by publishing deliberately overconfident predictions that he would win, Benchley deplored the public's taking such deceptions in high good humor: "It is this good-natured acceptance of having been bilked that makes the reading public worthy of more bilking."[27]

The writing of the "Guy Fawkes" column was part of Benchley's lifelong testimonial in favor of freedom of expression. In the *World* (July 19, 1920), Benchley wrote concerning Guy Emerson's *The New Frontier* that this book "will never be suppressed by the Department of Justice (although it does contain a seditious quotation from the Declaration of Independence)."

Robert then committed the same kind of sedition in *Of All Things!* by reprinting the first two paragraphs of the Declaration as a "Preface." This gesture looked like nonsense humor because the paragraphs were irrelevant to anything else in the book, but actually it was an indirect blow in defense of reason during the period following the raids ordered by Attorney General Palmer in which many persons were thrown into jail on mere suspicion of Communist sympathies. As already noted, Benchley walked in a picket line for Sacco and Vanzetti, testified against Judge Thayer, who had sentenced them to death, and praised the inclusion by Thurber and by Elliot Nugent of "academic freedom and Bartolomeo Vanzetti's letter" in *The Male Animal.*[28]

Believing as he did that official suppression was a greater risk than the permission of license, Benchley deplored the legal action taken against James Branch Cabell's *Jurgen* by the Society for the Suppression of Vice; yet he himself criticized the book as sharply as he did the censors. "Of course it was silly to suppress 'Jurgen'," he affirmed. "But it seems equally silly, because of its being suppressed, to hail it as high art. It is simply Mr. James Branch Cabell's quaint way of telling a raw story."[29] Benchley's moderation about this novel earned him "sneers from literati and cries of 'Philistine'" from readers of his column in the *World;* but he was defended by a fellow humorist, Oliver Herford, who pointed out that, unlike another eminent reviewer, Benchley was not actually proposing to put the book to a moral test for purposes of possible suppression.[30]

Without pretending to solve their quarrel, Benchley preferred to attack both the prudish and the prurient through satire. He parodied *Jurgen,* and in "Drama Cleansing and Pressing" (from *Pluck and Luck*) he averred that, "A pretty good way to judge in advance about the intrinsic art of a sex play is to see whether the characters have a good time at it or not. If they get fun out of the thing, then it's a harmful play. If they hate it, it's a work of art" (268). Benchley then offered three parodies of a potentially naughty triangle situation. The first, a light-hearted bedroom scene, is supposed to be wicked; the second, a parody of O'Neill's *Desire Under the Elms,* is supposed to be moral. The scene is "A bedroom in a cold New England farmhouse. The only light comes from the ice in the wash-pitcher." Eben enters (271).

[70]

Eben: Whar's Ezra?
Hilda: Out in the barn, torturing the horses.
Eben: That's good. Mebbe I kin tell yer now, Hilda, how much I love yer.
Hilda: That'd be fine, Eben. *(Punches herself on the jaw. Eben kisses her and they both cry.)*

The third parody in this set is aimed at playgoers who dislike frank dialogue. In this "acceptable" version, words like "Whadye-call it," "thingamabob," and "whatzis" predominate; and Benchley (who personally abstained from dirty words and responded coldly to obscene jokes) thus saved his last dart for the prudes. He felt that dramatic and literary dirt should be neither pitied nor censored.

VI *Little Man and Militant Citizen*

A myth for which American humorists themselves are partly responsible is that their humor cannot deal with important political and social matters. Mark Twain proclaimed himself just a funnyman and was irked when people took him for no more than that. Thurber declared that what happened to the axle of his car, his digestion, and his personal relationships was more important than what went on in the nation or in the universe.[31] Benchley once called himself "simply a person who writes little articles sporadically, and with no distinction."[32] Believing the author rather than his work, readers tend to overlook the large vein of social satire in the output of such humorists, even when these writers exchange the mask of meek bumbler for that of the active, indignant citizen.

Whenever he faced the facts about discrimination against Negroes, Benchley abandoned parody, farce, and sometimes the mask of the Little Man. Before World War I he gave some time to the Urban League, but after the war he seems to have rediscovered the problem of Negro oppression, less through the news about race riots or about the revival of the Ku Klux Klan than through reading two books, *Darkwater* by W. E. B. DuBois and *The Negro Faces America* by Herbert J. Seligman.[33] With scorn and irony Benchley attacked "the complacent quiet which usually reigns around this problem of America," and the hypocritical chauvinism which reigned during the war.

Said Benchley:

> Mr. Du Bois seems overwrought. Perhaps during the war he heard of the bloody crimes of our enemies, and saw preachers and editors and statesmen stand aghast at the barbaric atrocities which won for the German the name of Hun, and then looked toward his own people and saw them being burned, disembowelled and tortured with a civic unanimity and tacit legal sanction which made the word Hun sound weak.

Benchley then made this point: "Instead of taking over the protectorate of Armenia, we might better take over a protectorate of the State of Georgia, which yearly leads the proud list of lynchers."

He comments on Seligman's book by presenting himself as a dilatory reviewer cleaning up his back reading of light books by Mary Heaton Vorse,[34] Kathleen Norris, J. S. Fletcher and Sax Rohmer, and finally opening the Seligman volume:

> And suddenly the week-end, and the niceties of bringing up little white children to be ladies and gentlemen, and "Harriet and the Piper" and "The Paradise Mystery" in the Gloucester hammock all became very small indeed, and the white-flannelled groups waiting in shining motor-cars at the stations as we flashed through seemed singularly offensive and unnecessary.

How is it, he asked in the same review, that everyone is not exclusively concerned with "the most elementary, the most bitter injustice" meted out to thousands of Negro children? The answer followed in the form of bitter self-mockery:

> But I found them waiting for me to make a fourth at tennis, and then, what with one thing and another, it was bedtime, and I read "The Golden Scorpion" before I went to sleep, and the next day was Sunday and of course nothing could be done on Sunday, and soon my conscience became a little less restive and has improved rapidly since then.

Into this portrayal of himself as middle-class lout, Benchley worked criticism of fluffy reading, of public apathy, and possibly of Christian hypocrisy. His personal guilt-feeling was completely genuine; in reply to a criticism of the Harlem *Amsterdam News* that, in calling for more plays in which Negroes had "to behave as sensibly as white folk," he had cast a slur on the Negro people,[35] he stated at length that he was opposing the depiction on stage of Negro stereotypes.[36] Earlier he had hailed the performance of the Negro actor Charles Gilpin in O'Neill's *The Emperor Jones* as indicative that Negro performers had long since been ready "for more serious work than rolling dice in a musical comedy or limping about with lumbago after 'de young mars' Godfrey.' "[37]

His use of the term "race" and his reference to the "native genius for emotional expression" possessed by the Negro suggest that Benchley had not cleared quite all stereotyped ideas out of his own mind. Be that as it may, he attacked objectors to the miscegenation theme in *All God's Chillun Got Wings*,[38] and he exploded when the Theatre Guild relegated a Negro to the balcony.[39] In joining the army of humorists who made merry over President Harding's puddly prose, Benchley presented the Emancipation Proclamation as Harding might have written it, and more than mere style was satirized in Benchley's "I am first of all, for justice to the negroes and equally first of all, for justice to the slave-owners."[40]

As Thurber said, Benchley's "Wayward Press" pieces and his casuals "often had a club handy to the end."[41] The wielder was then a crusading variant of the *bonum vir,* the good plain man of Horace, Juvenal, Pope, Swift, Bierce, and Mencken. Much of the time, however, Benchley stayed behind the mask of the bumbler, even in moments of high indignation. Sometimes a pun or other quirk irrelevant to the subject hinted that the indignant voice came from an irresponsible fellow after all—"It was Taine (of 'Taine Goin' to Rain No More') who said: 'Democracies defeat themselves. Perhaps I haven't got that quotation right. It doesn't seem to mean much."[42]

Sometimes the anger of the author behind the narrator was partly veiled by an overt laughing of the narrator at himself, as in the second half of the above passage. Sometimes this veiling was done more thoroughly by self-caricature too fantastic to be taken seriously, as when Benchley attacked the misuse of credit by governments and by large corporations:

> I sign a check, in a kidding way, and give it to Altmeyer's Meat Market. And what does Altmeyer do? Right away he *pre-*

sents it at my bank! And then hell breaks loose. Telephone-calls, registered letters, night-sweats—you'd think the whole world had gone money-mad. And I have to go and get a printing-press and *print* him his money in half a day."[43]

By 1930 Benchley was beginning to tire of writing humor. He pounded out pieces for another ten years, including some of his best; but he wrote less social commentary than he had in the 1920's. However, the meekness and frustration of the Little Man as fixed in print mainly by Benchley made this figure readily adaptable by other writers as an agent for airing the economic and social problems that baffled Americans during the "angry decade." In contrast to the decline in effectiveness of Mencken's cocksure iconoclast, the Little Man grew during the 1930's partly because he was not tied too closely to any one writer's presuppositions and partly because the sources of his bedevilment—gadgets, political bunkum, the mass media, suburban life, sex, the family, and the brutal complexity of modern living—transcended the differences between prosperity and slump. Thurber, White, Perelman, Frank Sullivan, Wolcott Gibbs, and Russell Maloney were among the younger writers who followed Benchley in making the Little Man deal with social and economic realities as well as with more personal ones.

VII *Idols of the Lab*

Theoretical and applied science gave Benchley's bumbler the fidgets no less than did business and bureaucracy. Benchley was also augmenting a tradition in American humor of suspicion by the plain man toward any phenomenon tainted by intellect. The genial Clarence Day and the irascible Mr. Mencken were friendly toward the physical sciences because of their interest in theories of evolution; but John Kendrick Bangs, Harry Leon Wilson, Finley Peter Dunne, Don Marquis, and James Thurber confessed their befuddlement by numbers and formulas, and voiced their distrust of laboratories.[44]

The almost standardized attitude of humorists in Benchley's generation was that science should be dismissed as esoteric humbug unless it met the tests of common-sense and of humanity. There were two such tests: (1) however mysterious any scientific topic or technical device might be, it must be explainable in ordinary English; and (2) it must have a clear relation to human experience outside the laboratory or away from the drawing board. Marquis felt that statistics were utterly divorced from empirical reality; Thurber spoke for sensory experience and against what he felt was the scientists' dread of every-day reality when he claimed that they were "afraid of bloodhounds" and devoted themselves to the "inanimate and the impalpable."[45]

Benchley, too, disliked the abstracting, narrowing tendencies among scientists; but he sprayed his most corrosive acids on the unintelligibility of scientific writing, displaying even less tolerance than when he found its counterpart elsewhere. Shortly after Einstein had used the opportunity afforded by a total eclipse to demonstrate that gravity (in this case, the gravitational field of the sun) could and did "bend" light rays, Benchley impersonated and caricatured an ordinary reader struggling with Einstein's explanation:

> A ray of light is deflected by gravitation, the amount of deflection being twice that predicated by the electromagnetic theory. That puts it right up to the electromagnetic theory. Once you find out what that is, and have multiplied it by two, and then shuffled the pack as many times as you desire, it will be found that all the flags of the Allies are tied together, with Old Glory in the middle.

Remember, though, that there are two systems of relativity, the special and the general. "They are both really the same, except that one is a little larger than the other and doesn't scan so evenly." Moreover, Mr. Einstein raises complex questions which he does not answer—just like a German. "If only this discovery could have been made by a representative of one of the friendly Allies."[46]

The narrator gets three contexts—physics, cards, and international politics—absurdly confused. Through such caricature Benchley keeps his attack in the realm of farce. The criticism of anyone who tries to explain one set of phenomena by reference to another set equally inexplicable—the electromagnetic theory— appeals not to farce, however, but to common-sense.

Benchley liked the life sciences no better than the physical sciences, but nearly all of his pieces about either are also pegs for satire of other aspects of human pretentiousness—aspects both related and unrelated to science. In "The Social Life of the Newt" (from *Of All Things!*) and in "Polyp with a Past" (from *Love Conquers All*), Benchley parodied both the personifications of popularizers ("Thus, little creature, did your romance end.") and their attempts to lend spurious erudition to their prose through reference to German sources: "Until the valuable researches by Strudlehoff in 1887 (in his *'Entwickelungsmechanik'*) ..." Discoursing on the newt, Benchley digs at overemphasis on sex and also at the prudishness of many writers and editors.[47]

Some of the crackerbox oracles went soft on science when its theories were applied practically; the outcome of Will Rogers' interest in aviation, for example, is well known. But if one thing irked Benchley more than popular hypnosis concerning some incomprehensible aspect of scientific theory, it was ballyhoo about "practical" applications of science. For example, he had nothing against Byrd and Lindbergh personally, but he soon got very tired of the publicity about what he regarded as mainly stunts by these fliers. After Byrd's flight over the North Pole in 1926, Benchley wrote a series of parodies (most of which apeared in *The Early Worm*) about "The *Life* Polar Expedition," in which a group of bumblers, including himself and "Lieut.-Commander Marc Connelly," set off for the Pole on bicycles. Robert's annoyance at journalistic gush about the Lindbergh, Chamberlain, and Byrd transatlantic flights also crackled in the early columns of "The Wayward Press."[48]

Considering Benchley's bafflment by "the hundred and one little bits of wood and metal that go to make up the impedimenta of our daily life—the shoes and pins, the picture books and door keys, the bits of fluff and sheets of newspaper"[49]—one might dismiss his hostility toward the automobile, airplane, telephone, and radio as sour grapes. But, as hinted earlier, he usually broadened his satire in his anti-technical pieces to include aspects of personal or institutional behavior. Thus, in "Lesson Number One" (from *Of All Things!*), inspired by his single disastrous attempt to drive a car unassisted, Benchley directed his fire at the tendency of the common man to parade his half-knowledge and to rationalize his ignorance. In pieces on science and technology, one of Benchley's main points is always that these fields offer peculiar temptations to egotism.

VIII   *Doctors under the Knife*

Benchley had a sharp scalpel for medicine men, especially psychiatrists, psychoanalysts, and their allies among authors and journalists. Medical doctors have been fairly frequent targets in American humor—the incompetent Dr. Cuticle in Herman Melville's *Whitejacket* has plenty of company, especially in humor of the frontier.[50] Moreover, medicine progressed until (as one scientist quipped) it reached the point where "a random patient with a random disease consulting a physician at random stood better than a 50-50 chance of benefiting from the encounter."[51] With progress came increasing use of medical services; and, with more use, still more humor. Mr. Dooley and Mr. Leacock poked fun at medical jargon, overspecialization, and high fees; Irvin S. Cobb and Will Rogers squirmed verbally under the surgeon's knives.[52]

Benchley did more than squirm; he grew feathers. When a doctor prescribed one of the new sulfa drugs for him, Robert and the actor Charles Butterworth broke open a pillow and used library paste to coat the patient all over with feathers, from the waist down. When the doctor asked if the sulfa had done any good, Benchley said "Is this all right?" and threw back the bedclothes.[53] In life, the Little Man as patient had struck back.

In his writing, Benchley also took the side of the patient. "How to Avoid Colds," in *From Bed to Worse*, included the suggestion that a surgeon would be delighted to stick into one's throat a gadget for supplying one with air. "Most of us get too much air anyway." Of medical research Benchley was so suspicious that he and his persona almost became one and the same. Speaking "straight," as a drama critic, Benchley criticized the ruthlessness of the doctors in Sidney Howard's *Yellow Jack* who experimented on people. Speaking as Little Man in two satires on American medical research in Africa, Benchley absurdly twisted a few facts but was eminently sane in scoring the excessive publicity, the slack methodology, and the paternalism which, he felt, characterized these projects.[54]

The naïve wise fool in *No Time for Sergeants* who shattered the aplomb of a psychiatrist had ancient and honorable precedent. As far as I can find, Benchley was the second primarily humorous writer in America to include psychology and its branches among his major themes. Oliver Wendell Holmes having been the first. Not, of course, until the science became a major discipline could it become a major target in humor. G. Stanley Hall had founded the *American Journal of Psychology* in 1887, and William James published *Principles of Psychology* in 1890; thereafter, John Kendrick Bangs, Frank Moore Colby, Clarence Day, Jr., and others took sharp but infrequent pokes at the new field. Freud had lectured in America in 1908; translation of his works began shortly afterward; and, by the early 1920's all disciplines labeled "psych" were trickling steadily into the public mind through works by Hall, Havelock Ellis, and less careful popularizers.

Benchley satirized two of these popularizers in the *World*. As a harried citizen trying to figure his income tax, the reviewer criticizes *Psychoanalysis* by André Tridon. As a generally neurotic bumbler, he ridicules *The Problem of Nervous Breakdown*, by Edwin L. Ash:

> In the chapter on "Morbid Fears and Doubts" we see what science can do in the elevation of homely emotions to the status of classical diseases. We also recognize several little eccentricities of our own classed among the "phobias" which are evidently but preliminary sounds to the general breaking-up of the ice in our mental river, it being only a question of time before they reduce us to the state where we have to be helped away, passing our hands vaguely before our eyes and muttering, "Don't let them get at me."[55]

Benchley's narrator is absurd only in being, like most people, insecure enough to fall a too-easy victim to the persuasions of the analyst that he is neurotic. He is quite sane, really—essentially sane, or three-quarters sane, or as sane as most people; and who can hope for more? This stance of the Sane Neurotic is assumed by Benchley in such better-known pieces as "Phobias" and "All Aboard for Dementia Praecox" (both in *My Ten Years in a Quandary*) in which he admits to defective judgment, retarded perception, lack of skill in motor performance, and stupor: "I can say only that there are hundreds of people willing to bet that I have *never* had my eyes open. I have no proof to the contrary." By implication, the analysts have no proof for their assumptions.[56]

Benchley agreed with William James that psychology was not a science.[57] Perhaps the specialists had taken greater leave of common-sense than had the patient.

In general, five images of the scientist have predominated in popular culture. One is the sinister, insane genius, such as "Ivan Eviloff" in the comic strip "Dan Dunn," and Zarkov in "Flash Gordon" before Flash tamed him. A second is the absent-minded potterer, such as Dr. Huer in "Buck Rogers." The third is the wizard or magician: Dos Passos in *U.S.A.* shows how Edison and Steinmetz were re-created as such by high-voltage publicity. The fourth image gained some ground during the 1920's and 1930's: that of the scientist as a quietly dedicated public servant. Paul de Kruif, Sinclair Lewis, and Sidney Kingsley helped to popularize this type. The fifth and most recent image is that of the astronaut as research worker, explorer, and hero.

The image of the scientist portrayed in sophisticated humor has basically resembled none of these types, though it has points of similarity with the absent-minded figure. However, the Dr. Huer type is also a scientific wonder who is seldom wrong within his specialty, whereas Benchley followed Bangs, Cobb, and Dunne—and preceded Thurber, White, and Perelman —in persistently hinting that the scientist was a bumbling Milquetoast as wrongheaded within his field as out of it. In the case of the psychiatrist, the image first vividly etched by Benchley has become a staple. The crop of "headshrinker" jokes and stories probably owes something to the evil-genius image, but it surely owes much to the sane psychoses of Robert Benchley.

IX   *The Little Man and the Arts*

Concerning literature and the fine arts, Benchley's spokesman refracts his creator's university background in the humanities, that is, he is never philistine, but neither is he "arty" or *avant garde* (Benchley the man, of course, was a professional playgoer and critic during much of his career. He had scholarly interests too, having for years collected notes on the humor of the Queen Anne period).[58] He doesn't let scholars and critics come between him and the work of art; he is an amateur who reads for pleasure, not a professional reader.

His tastes in reading were on a somewhat higher brow-level—high enough that he sometimes tried to conceal them from his associates. He kept his more erudite books hidden in the closet—"books in German, books on philosophy, books on obscure subjects, books on music—which he didn't especially want people to know that he was reading. He read all the time, sometimes being into four or five books at once; but he was so afraid of appearing pretentious that he would occasionally, particularly in Hollywood, cover a volume of Proust with the dust jacket from a murder mystery."[59] This conduct fits his pose in print as a middlebrow bumbler. Yet, in order to express his dislike of James Joyce and William Faulkner and to parody Proust, Dreiser, Mencken, Nathan, Cabell, O'Neill, and many other writers, Benchley had to present his *alter ego* as familiar with some of their works. The Little Man could not claim, with Will Rogers, that "All I know is what I read in the papers."[60]

Actually, Robert, as an undergraduate at Harvard, doggedly read clear through Dr. Eliot's Five-Foot Shelf of great books; but, long before he had finished, he decided that many of the so-called classics were living on their reputation. In a key essay, "Mind's Eye Trouble" (from *No Poems*), his persona implies a declaration of literary independence which was no pretense; but the fictitious Benchley does pretend that his independence is forced on him by "a paucity of visual imagination" which causes him to substitute his own boyhood environment for whatever setting any author has used: "Regardless of what Hugo had in mind, *I* have Front Street, Worcester, in mind when I read it" [*Les Miserables*]. He even finds himself "sending Proust walking up and down the street with Albertine." Absurd? This statement is merely an exaggeration of a tendency in a great many readers as well as a condensed version, not at all exaggerated, of the quite respectable critical view that all great works are contemporary. Rightly or wrongly, the normal bumbler demands, as the price of the authors' survival, that literary "greats" from Julius Caesar to Katherine Mansfield give him people and events meaningful within his own frame of reference.

Elsewhere, Benchley's narrator suggests the same standard in claiming that most of Shakespeare is dead because modern actors cannot make him effective, and "You can't blame the actor entirely." Shakespearean comedy in particular is "horsy and crass." Conversely, modern readers pose too great a challenge for Shakespeare; and the reader who has not remained the intellectual slave of his schoolteachers will read him in snatches and *stop* reading when he feels like it. In "Shakespeare Explained" (from *The Benchley Roundup*), Benchley parodied the assiduous annotators who load the text with futile footnotes; his ideal common reader is no scholar. But he is well-read, and his reactions to literature are more sincere and therefore more genuinely appreciative than the reactions of the professors who must often be classed with the psychoanalysts, bankers, and other aggressive boobs of the upper-middle class who bedevil the Little Man.

Painting and sculpture are not often mentioned in Benchley's writing, although there is one piece on African sculptures—"I wouldn't give them houseroom."[61] Benchley had a little more to say about classical music, not much of it friendly. "Music Heavenly Maid" (in *Chips Off the Old Benchley*) depicts the difficulty of the Little Man as writer who is trying to work while the next-door neighbors listen to the philharmonic on the radio. Music in the Schönberg manner and its over-interpreters get a severe ribbing: "What you think are random noises made by the musicians falling over forward on their instruments, are, when you understand them, really steps in a great, moving story—the Story of the Traveling Salesman who came to the Farm-house." "Opera Synopses" and "More Songs for Meller" satirize nonmusical aspects of grand opera and song recitals, respectively.[62]

These examples do not add up to disliking good music, but "I have nothing against symphonies"[63] is the strongest statement in their favor made by the Benchley persona. Like Ade and Lardner, Benchley was definitely indifferent to grand opera; but he keenly appreciated musical comedy and the songs of vaudeville. At Harvard, Benchley belonged to the Mandolin Club, and later on he, like Lardner, would join informal sing-songs around the piano any old time. Unquestionably, his preferences in music harmonized with those of many of his readers.

A correlative of the Little Man's independence is his isolation, a problem also affecting mass-man but for somewhat different reasons. The Little Man is emotionally cut off from those who harass him, and his harassers are cut off from each other. Although isolation is seldom stressed in Benchley's pieces, it underlies many of them and breaks the surface here and there, usually in an emphasis on the breakdown of communication between man and man. Explanations of Shakespeare, relativity, cell division, finance, and football do not explain anything; Paul Revere yells something nobody understands;[64] the Treasurer reports nothing except that he is competent to report nothing.

Moreover, to indicate preoccupation with self, Benchley's people interrupt and disrupt each others' trains of alleged thought; children are either incoherently noisy or too quiet: "All I can figure out is that they are plotting a revolution."[65] Benchley's anti-hero is not so wholly locked within himself as the typical Lardner character, whose main problem may be one of communication, in a broad sense of the term. But Benchley's type-figure is badly enough off to remind one of Thurber's Mr. Monroe and Walter Mitty, and even of Eliot's Prufrock who seldom tries to communicate with anyone because he is afraid he'll be told "That is not what I meant, at all."[66] Benchley's man is in a large and lonely crowd.

CHAPTER *6*

Benchley on Humor

E B. WHITE has written that "Humor can be dissected, as a frog can, but the thing dies in the process."[1] Benchley felt much the same way; yet he had quite a bit to say about certain aspects of humor, and because much of his theory was a rationalization of his practice, his essays and scattered comments on humor throw light on some of his themes and techniques as well as on his limitations.

I *"Brow-Elevation"*

The closest Benchley came to defining humor was a hint that it depended much upon conventions shared by the humorist and his public: A joke is funny only if the jokester and his audience think it is. This view was not exactly original, nor was his feeling that analyzing a quip kills it and that"The chances are that the person to whom you have been explaining it won't think that it is funny anyway."[2] Benchley implied that if the audience is larger than one, the likelihood of humorous conventions being entirely shared decreases proportionately. Naturally he took a dim view of Max Eastman's analytical, not to say psychoanalytical, approach in *Enjoyment of Laughter;* and in a parody of that book he suggested that laughter is really caused by a small tropical fly carried from Central America to Spain by Columbus's men, "returning to America, on a visit, in 1667, on a man named George Altschuh."[3]

Conceivably, Benchley was also irked by Eastman's just criticisms that his own humor was sometimes wordy and labored; in addition, he certainly shared the instinctive repulsion felt by many humorists at being picked apart by scholars, regardless of the slant or "school" of approach. Humor was supposed to be fun. It should also involve a laugh *with* rather than *at* its object;

here Benchley agreed wholeheartedly with Leacock, an agreement natural in a humorist who likewise poked a great deal of fun at himself.[4] Yet Benchley resembled Mark Twain in disliking the role of a mere funnyman whom no one would take seriously. He worried about writing something "Really Good" that would contribute to Progress,[5] rated humor, including his own, outside the category of good writing, and thought of it mainly as a vehicle of entertainment rather than of enlightenment. The contradiction between his low rating of his calling and his gusto in the pursuit of it was never resolved. Yet this conflict may have had something to do with his occasional spurts of biting social satire and his uncharacteristic outburst at a party against Robert E. Sherwood just after the latter had won the second of his three Pulitzer prizes.[6]

In his "funning," Benchley, on the whole, preferred metropolitan subtlety to crossroads crudity. Of Frank Crowninshield he wrote: "As a boy he conceived a bitter dislike for the joke in which a fat man is shown sitting down on a bench marked 'Fresh Paint.'... Humor which needs gesticulation and powerful wrinklings of the visage for its best effect leaves him mirthless."[7] Benchley too voiced his scorn for those who laugh when someone slips on a banana peel. He also disliked the crude misuse of words and the inverted anti-intellectual snobbery of the crackerbox oracles.[8] Leo Marx has said that the uncombed American vernacular, shaped into a great literary medium by Whitman and Mark Twain, was more than a literary technique; it was "a view of experience"—a view narrowed by anti-intellectualism.[9] Benchley and the contemporary humorists whom he respected— for example, Stephen Leacock and Franklin P. Adams—were trying to intellectualize the vernacular (one might say) and thus to broaden the American experience.

To Benchley, however, intellectualized, or "high-brow," humor involved much more than use or non-use of the vernacular. In *The Seven Lively Arts* (1924) Gilbert Seldes had praised Lardner, Irving Berlin, the stage comic Joe Cook, and the creator of "Krazy Kat," George Herriman. Benchley commented on Seldes' views thus:

> To us it is quite understandable that Mr. Seldes, a highbrow,
> should revel genuinely and without affectation in the work of
> Lardner, Cook, Berlin and Herriman, because these gentlemen

are Grade-A highbrows themselves. Each has a universal quality which renders him popular, but at his best he is so far over the heads of the average reader and audience that he might as well be working in a foreign medium.

Lardner's entire structure is built on an unsparing and sophisticated exposure of the lowbrow mind, so subtle and delicate that thousands of readers of the *Saturday Evening Post* unquestionably found nothing amusing in it except the quite adventitious misspelling and slang. Messrs. Cook and Herriman are entirely mad at heart, and sheer madness is, of course, the highest possible brow in humor. They have, just as Ring Lardner has, certain fundamental comic elements which make everybody laugh, regardless of brow-elevation, but in the upper reaches of their imagination they are for only the sophisticates.[10]

On the other hand, Benchley classed Mencken's humor, Shakespearian comedy and the Russian ballet as lowbrow:

Mr. Mencken, while sophisticated enough for all practical purposes in his mental processes and serious criticism, is, when he wants to be funny, dependent on the extremely lowbrow medium of comic-sounding words like "pish-posh" and *"sitz-platz,"* and figures of speech reminiscent of Public School 165 when sitting down heavily and kicking in the seat of the pants were considered good enough fun for anyone. When Mr. Mencken has said something funny to you it is all over your face like a pail of whitewash, and he has nothing left for himself.

The comedy of the Russians and Shakespeare, with its concomitant cheek-blowing and grunting, is comparable with the Mencken method in tonnage, but is without Mr. Mencken's mature intent. It all is derived from the whitewash pail and all is particulary delightful to auditors under eight years of age or their equivalent.[11]

Benchley's distinction between sophistication and mere erudition was as sound as his differentiation between "pratfall" humor and more sophisticated funmaking. However, for the sake of those "certain fundamental comic elements," Benchley sometimes combined the "pratfall" and the thoughtfully knitted highbrow. Just as Ignatz Mouse repeatedly beans Krazy Kat with a brick, Benchley's Uncle George stumbles over a child's electric train, Papa Benchley lunges at son Bobby and falls off his bicycle, and football fans find themselves frozen to their seats. All of these episodes illustrate a fundamental comic element that Benchley recognized but seldom bothered to summarize explicitly: the incongruity between what man is and what he ought to be. Thus, in context, his bits of low comedy also offer something to the thinking minority—to the custodians of George Meredith's "Comic Spirit" and to the sort of readers Harold Ross hoped for. The first two of the examples just cited from Benchley's work are taken from parodies of Dickens and of "scientific" journalists, respectively; the third is from a critique of the mob-man as football fan.[12] In all three, and elsewhere, Benchley simply ignores his own theoretical distinctions.

One type of humor for the thoughtful was, Benchley felt, "a broad burlesquing of modern entertainment formulae and clichés, with a strain of pleasant insanity running through the whole." In 1926 he found this kind of humor in "certain New York supperclubs" that were sponsoring "a crazy and highly amusing form of comedy, miles and miles in advance of the conventional revue stuff."[13] Jimmy Durante, for instance, "mystifies some, irritates others, and provides incomparable entertainment for those whose minds swing free and loose and who are sick unto death of the old forms." In other words, this "greatest of all madmen" appealed mainly to connoisseurs, as did Joe Cook, whose praises Benchley also sang.[14] Unfortunately, Benchley seldom quoted or described their material, but, in 1924, Edmund Wilson too had noticed "the revolution in humor that seems to be taking place in New York." Wilson stressed the "nonsense of Joe Cook and Robert Benchley" as part of this revolution, and recounted, "Joe Cook asks 'the Senator,' his stooge, 'How's your uncle?'—and the Senator answers, 'I haven't got an uncle.' 'Fine,' says Cook, 'How is he?'"[15]

Like this rather flat bit, Cook's nonsense was presented mostly for laughs and was devoid of satire, as was much of the earlier buffoonery of the Marx brothers. Benchley, whose mind swung free and loose before he discovered Cook, went beyond the stage comedians in controling his "insanity" for purposes of parody. Thus, he put a deaf elk and a woman weaving tapestry together into a greenhouse in order to parody amateur analysts of dreams. To parody art songs, as represented by their vapid synopses in program notes, Benchley mixed personification and nonsequitur:

It is the day of the bull fight in Madrid. Everyone is cockeyed. The bull has slipped out by the back entrance to the arena and has gone home, disgusted. Nobody notices that the bull has gone except Nina, a peasant girl who has come to town that day to sell her father. She looks with horror at the place in the Royal Box where the bull ought to be sitting, and sees there instead her algebra teacher, whom she had told that she was staying at home on account of a sick headache. You can imagine her feelings![16]

Bullfighting and the sentimentalizing over quaint peasant mores also get hit here. Thus Benchley combined nonsense, topical satire, and parody.

Much of the supper-club humor was in the form of parody, and most of Benchley's pieces were, or included, parody (or burlesque, to use the term he preferred). For example, seven of the first ten pieces in *The Benchley Roundup* are parodies of "modern entertainment formulae and clichés," and two of the remaining three may be so considered ("Take the Witness!" and "The Tortures of Week-End Visiting"). Five of the pieces are almost exclusively parody. In print, parody undiluted by author comment is the equivalent of oral delivery with a poker face, and Benchley delivered most of his oral monologues with a face like a graven image. Of a man who died laughing at his own joke, Benchley said, "If he had given it with a dead pan he would have been alive today and would have been visiting me in New York at my expense."[17]

But to enjoy fully this form of humor—parody—the receiver must share a common body of knowledge and feelings with the parodist, perhaps more fully than is required with other forms of humor. To get the most out of Benchley's parodies, one should have absorbed nature-study lectures, Shakespearean scholarship, Dickensian sentimentality, the drab realism of certain twentieth-century novels, and some specialized papers like those published by the American Psychiatric Association. Benchley's part in the "revolution," as summarized by Edmund Wilson, included much parody of the more complex and intellectual forms of communication and "entertainment," and relatively little lunacy for its own sake.

II *The Poker Face, Pathos, and Other Matters*

Not caring whether he was a "revolutionary" in humor or not,

Benchley insisted on a commonplace: humor must convey the effect of spontaneity. This humorist, who sweated over his own writing, felt that such an· effect required presentation in one's own language, "freshness" (up-to-dateness), and, preferably, understatement. As a result, he was cold to humor in translation or in the English of previous periods, such as the ages of Shakespeare, Queen Anne, and Mark Twain. (His collection of notes for a study of humor of the Queen Anne period was begun partly as proof that he could do some "serious" writing and was abandoned when he finally decided that no humorist of this period was funny.[18]) His already mentioned preference for the cultivated Franklin P. Adams instead of Mark Twain's dialect humor was part of his demand that humor be up-to-date. Freshness was also needed in the handling of character types, situations, and jokes; but on this topic Benchley found it easier to say what he didn't like than what he liked.

His theater reviews are seasoned with sarcasms about trite material, and in "Visitors' Day at the Joke Farm"[19] certain character types associated with stock situations reminisce at the "Home for Aged Jokes"—the grandiloquent old actor, the comic tramp, and the Broadway dandy—exchange memories with the missionary who was always being cooked by cannibals ·and with the man who was always kicking a hat on the sidewalk that had a brick in it. In the background hover Alkali Ike the cowboy, Willie Tenderfoot; the Irate Father who calls "Lydia, hasn't that young man gone yet?"; and the little girl who asks "Muvver, what did Daddy mean when he said—." In "Old Wives' Tale," the author scoffs at early versions of the henpecked husband theme that included the throwing of dishes and the use of the rolling-pin.[20] In both essays, much of the humor of *Life, Puck,* and *Judge* at about the time of "Grover Cleveland and the Full Dinner-pail"[21] is explicitly rejected.

By "freshness" Benchley did not mean mere topicality. He did respect originality of situation; he thought Max Beerbohm's "Enoch Soames" was "an original idea, remarkably well told" and "the best short story I have ever read."[22] (The story concerns a bad poet who is granted a vision of the future; instead of experiencing the fame that he has confidently expected would be his, he stares into oblivion.) However, Benchley wrote best about the confused American who, during the early years of

Robert's career, was already becoming a stock figure on the stage (in 1920 and 1921 Benchley praised Ed Wynn and W. C. Fields for their portrayals of the bumbler[23]), and he wrote some of his most effective humor about this type-figure long after his earlier pieces had helped to make the Little Man a stock character in the humorous essay as well. To Benchley, freshness meant, in part, up-to-dateness in language, so that one of his objections to Shakespeare's comedy was that Elizabethan English was archaic and therefore dead. Accordingly, as a drama critic he was hard on Restoration and eighteenth-century comedy largely because, as he admitted, dialogue in a play simply had to be "in my own set" to be effective.

Besides freshness of language, another attribute that Benchley associated with up-to-dateness was understatement. Here, too, his practice deviated from his theory. He felt, however, that modern comedy was better than Shakespeare's because it had less noise, less mugging, and less cruelty. He therefore praised Charlie Chaplin for his frozen face, and he awarded palms to the cast of George M. Cohan's *The Tavern* for underplaying this "burlesque of romantic drama."[24] Although Benchley's attitude toward Chaplin vacillated—Nathaniel Benchley says that "He hated Chaplin. Called his humor 'rectal kicking' "[25]—he could hardly avoid taking an interest in Chaplin's playing of bumbler roles.

Again denying his own practice in part, Benchley felt that the subject matter of humor was severely limited. Although current social and political events like the Eighteenth Amendment, the Palmer raids, the Five-Year Plan, and the New Deal—along with the latest developments in science, technology, books, and drama—supplied most of the pegs for his humor, Benchley felt that only a rare specialist should try to be topical: "Our idea would be to leave all timely matters and quips on the news to Mr. Will Rogers, and have everyone else confine himself to being funny with the eternal verities and all that sort of deathless thing."[26] Despite his admiration for Rogers, Benchley preferred the wackiness of Fanny Brice and the clumsiness of W. C. Fields as he "fretted over the Ford."[27]

On topicality, Benchley stood in controversial territory. His position was close to that of Max Eastman; but Gilbert Highet, one of the more recent and readable commentators about humor and satire, feels that satire must be topical, although it should also be more than that.[28] But from "the eternal verities" with which humor was fit to deal, Benchley tended to subtract, as has been noted, not only the currently topical but the sexual and the obscene; as might be expected, his zest for up-to-date humor did not, therefore, include the bawdy, modern, or otherwise. He could be raffish in private and before restricted audiences—solemnly he informed a group of naval officers that prophylaxis after shore leave was to be made compulsory for officers as well as for enlisted men[29]—but to defenders of Rabelaisean humor in plays, he replied: " 'Rabelaisean humor' is dirty talk that Daddy can laugh at and not lose cast. 'Dirty talk' is what Junior gets spanked for."[30] The idea that children's conversation and Broadway plays might be different and not comparable media either did not occur or was not acceptable to him at the time.

True , he said of a show by Fred Stone, "There is such a thing as clean fun reaching a point of cleanliness where it is practically sterile," and he praised *Lysistrata* as a sex comedy that was both open and clean. Besides a categorical distaste for the hypocritical snigger, Benchley disliked triteness in the presentation of sex as of other themes: "Sex, as a theatrical property, is as tiresome as the Old Mortgage,"[31] he anounced in 1930, three years before *Tobacco Road* began its record-breaking run. Nonetheless, he offered no real defense for his theoretical exclusion of sex from humor; his queasiness seems entirely visceral, especially if viewed with Highet's observation in mind that much first-rate satire is redolent with sex and obscenity.[32]

One should note that Benchley's severities about the subject-matter of humor were typical of American columnists and essayists during the 1920's and 1930's. Public affairs was a major theme of only two outstanding humorists in these media, Will Rogers and E. B. White. Sex got somewhat more attention. White and Thurber asked, *Is Sex Necessary?* (1929) and decided that it was if other human problems received due weight; but the exploitation of sex by humorists in the shorter forms was slight compared to the slavering over this material by playwrights, by "serious" novelists, and by such writers of comic romances as James Branch Cabell, John Erskine, and Thorne Smith.[33]

Perhaps the greater freedom enjoyed by playwrights and novelists stimulated their literary sexuality. Writers in the shorter
forms labored under the restrictions of the newspapers and
magazines for which they wrote on salary, on assignment, or
as "free" lancers. *Vanity Fair* was too well-bred to get very dar-
ing; *Life* had allowed some naughtiness to creep into its illustrations around 1910 but thenceforth seldom sinned. Harold Ross
was no prude and rejected only incest and major blasphemy as
themes for humor;[34] but when Lardner, Benchley, Day, and
Marquis wrote for *The New Yorker*, they gave the editor little
trouble on the score of sexual liberality. On this subject they
were their own severest monitors. Either because they remained
prisoners of their Victorian childhoods or because they had been
too well trained during long careers under more timid editorial
chiefs than Ross, they easily sacrificed up-to-dateness for old-
fashioned reticence.

"I laugh," said Beaumarchais' Figaro, "that I need not weep."[35]
Benchley, too, belonged to the impressive band who have felt
that humor was very close to its opposite. Thurber said of
humorists that "The little wheels of their invention are set in
motion by the damp hand of melancholy,"[36] and Groucho Marx
retells the story of Grock, the clown, who went to a doctor
about his melancholia and was advised to go see Grock.[37]
Benchley admired "that approach to tragedy which marks great
comedy," and he respected Ed Wynn in part because "He has
that same aura of pathos which sublimates Charlie Chaplin and
makes him by turns a great comedian and a great tragedian."[38]

Yet Benchley made little use of pathos, a restraint that was
both good and bad. He never dragged tear-jerking situations
out of stock, as did Finley Peter Dunne in describing how a
fireman, killed in the collapse of a rickety building, was brought
home,[39] or as Lardner did in "There Are Smiles," where a flapper with a heart of gold and a weakness for reckless driving
was killed by the snap of an O. Henry ending.[40] On the other
hand, apart from the pieces in which he sprayed acid on social
injustices, Benchley's work suffers from excessive blandness. His
muse was not cankered enough; one misses the controlled pathos
and brooding melancholy that lend variety and tension to the
best writing of Lardner and Thurber.

Such darkness as there is in Benchley will receive its due in our discussion of his imagery. Meanwhile, as one ponders Highet's statements that excellent satire must be big, coarse, and hearty and that polite and sophisticated satires are "untypical, almost paradoxical,"[41] one wonders whether the *New Yorker* humorists were too thoroughly Benchleyized and even whether the entire trend of metropolitan humor and satire in the twentieth century has not veered from the main path marked by Chaucer, Boccaccio, Rabelais, Cervantes, Swift, and Fielding. Perhaps the suave, sophisticated moderns have laid out a new track; perhaps the "black humorists" of the angry, bawdy comic novel are the true "main-liners."

Whatever Benchley's limitations in theory and in practice, his comments on brow-elevation, spontaneity, the deadpan, social content, and sex not only link him with the older humorists of his generation but show his relationship to such younger, jumpier contemporaries as James Thurber, E. B. White, Wolcott Gibbs, and S. J. Perelman who further intellectualized the vernacular and made *The New Yorker* a magazine of distinction.

CHAPTER 7

Techniques: Mask,
Monologue, Dialogue

DESPITE Benchley's dim view of stock situations, he used many; but, under his careful polishing, they glittered with the effect of spontaneity. For example, there is the old theme of the man who has gulped an unexpectedly powerful drink:

> In about eight seconds the top of the inhaler's head rises slowly and in a dignified manner until it reaches the ceiling where it floats, bumping gently up and down. The teeth then drop out and arrange themselves on the floor to spell "Portage High School, 1930," the eyes roll upward and backward, and a strange odor of burning rubber fills the room.[1]

The bumping, the spelling, and the burning rubber are true Benchley touches—touches that revivify the old techniques of humorous exaggeration and of comic irony through overstatement. Every device and technique analyzed in this chapter was moss-grown before Benchley was born, but all of them—the Little Man mask, the incongruous yoking of contexts, irony of overstatement and understatement, and humorous imagery— sparkle with the "freshness" he prized.

I *The Mask as a Technique*

Content and form are fused in the Little Man. This character-type has been treated as subject matter, but whether he appears as suburbanite, father, writer, office worker, Innocent Abroad, playgoer ,or literary critic, he may also be treated as a technical device on which depend certain subordinate devices. These include kidding oneself and the *reductio ad absurdum*.

Poking fun at oneself is a standard way of disarming the reader, especially if he is actually being laughed at by the writer. In self-spoofing, Benchley usually stressed the littleness of his Little Man, that is, he exaggerated the author's own confusion. Readers might feels the same jitters and ineptitude, but to a less degree, and could reflect that they were, at any rate, superior to poor Benchley. When the bumbler rumbles that Mozart wrote no music until he was ninety and defends his mistake with "How was I to know that there were two Mozarts who were composers?,"[2] the reader may well recall similar but less flagrant mistakes of his own—like, perhaps, confounding the patriarchal Bach with some of his musical offspring.

Sometimes Benchley interrupted his self-satire to affirm openly instead of merely to imply his identity with readers. To the notion that man feels peppiest in spring, Benchley retorted that he himself had the most zip in the fall: "And I flatter myself that I am a member of that group which is known, euphemistically, as mankind. Not a member in very good standing, perhaps, but good enough to have a vote on the seasons"[3] (E. B. White also declared that he knew what was good for the common people because "I know what's good for me.").[4]

Often the mask is quickly restored, sometimes in the middle of a sentence. No sooner has Benchley proclaimed his membership in mankind and his right as an individual to his own experience than he invites the reader to dissociate himself from the speaker and to chuckle at that fool's temerity in thinking he could vote on how mankind behaves at which seasons. Also, the quick resumption of an absurd role eases the disagreement of any reader who fancies that *he* does feel better in the spring. The real target of the satire is the dogmatism of psychologists, the dogmatism of the Little Man being a caricature of theirs.

The same essay ("Those Dicta") is also an example of what might be termed the "reduction test." This variation of the *reductio ad absurdum* consists of a narrator in average circumstances but of more than average intelligence (for instance, a crackerbox oracle or a white-collared householder) who is pontificating absurdly on complex or esoteric matters. In so doing, he simplifies them to their essentials—reduces them to homely terms and situations that the man in the street can understand. The technique has been a staple of American humor: Lowell used it often in the *Biglow Papers* (as in "The Debate in the Sennit, Sot to a Nusry Rhyme"), and Mr. Dooley reduced the Dreyfus case to a Southside courtroom squabble ("'Jackuse' he [Zola] says. An' they thrun him out.")

The point may be that the shrewd, if ignorant, commentator has grasped the essentials of what merely seems complex (as in the case of Hosea Bigelow) or that the problems are too much for any layman and humility is in order ("That's all I know about Cap Dhry-fuss' case, an' that's all anny man knows.").[5] In either example, the common-man-as-thinker knows enough not to generalize beyond his experience. A classic American of this order is Huck Finn to whom slavery was not a set of high-flown abstractions but a specific demand that he betray his friend.

Benchley's point in applying the reduction test is likewise that every man should check pronouncements by "experts" and public oracles against his own experience. To any dictum of scientists, "At least three exceptions can be found right in my own house,"[6] and "The trouble with the specialists in what mankind does or does not do is that they don't get around enough with mankind."[7] Speaking in his crotchety way for mankind, the Little Man in this same volume, *My Ten Years in a Quandary*, draws on his own experience to test the experts on swimming, dogs, hiccoughs, Egyptology, dreams, economics, psychosis, statistics, dietetics, language, and assorted natural sciences including medicine and politics. The frequent absurdity of the narrator's sweeping inferences from his own limited experience merely makes his criticism humorous, without vitiating it as criticism. Concluding that "A still better way to develop the child is to have *it* hold the male relative" (200) in no way invalidates the Little Man's discovery that certain instructions of the baby-care specialists are equally absurd.

Sometimes, instead of attacking the experts, Benchley's man defends them in a fashion their worst enemies would never use. Walter Blair calls this time-honored weapon of burlesque the "numbskull" technique. Benjamin Franklin satirized the pro-slavery argument in 1790 by putting it into the mouth of an Arab defending the enslavement of Christians. During the Civil War, David Ross Locke propagandized for the Union by putting a defense of the Confederacy into the mouth of a stupid, venal character, Petroleum Vesuvius Nasby. In *My Ten Years in a*

Quandary Benchley spoofed writers and readers who take astronomical predictions too seriously by making his persona extremely pompous and gullible in foretelling showers of meteorites (91-4); and he criticized grammarians of the stuffy-genteel sort by pretending to be an inept member of that tribe—"Whom am I? (for where am I)" is one of the Little Man's corrections of the common man's English. In the field of international relations, Benchley burlesqued the Dawes plan by having his *alter ego* offer a plan for Germany's reparations which would result in the following account:

Total indemnity	3,000 000 000 marks
Total indemnity	6,000 000 000 marks
Total indemnity	11,000 000 000 marks
Total indemnity	8,000 000 000 marks[8]

II *Monologue and Dialogue*

Gilbert Highet says that satire has three main shapes: parody, non-parodic monologue, and "non-parodic fiction (dramatic or narrative)."[9] In discussing Benchley's techniques, one finds it simpler to think of parody not as a shape or form so much as an ingredient found to some degree in almost everything he wrote. Within the loose frame of the familiar essay, his basic "shapes" were the dramatic monologue, dialogue, and narrative; but the most important is the dramatic monologue, often given as a comic lecture.

Highet feels that the monologue of self-exposure is ultimately a trick of the theater, and Constance Rourke noted how, in the 1920's, the monologues of Sherwood Anderson and Ring Lardner suggested the improvisation of the oral talk or tale.[10] In high school and at Phillips Exeter Academy, Benchley had belonged to the dramatic clubs; at Harvard he had acted in several productions and had written his first drama criticism. His most effective humorous efforts at Cambridge had been his parody of a professor's lecture, his Ivy Oration, and the improvised talks in which he often impersonated a returned traveler or a politician—and generally reduced his audience to a "quivering shambles."[11]

Most of his early sallies into entertainment were by way of the stage or platform, and in dozens of his better essays he wrote like the monologuist and actor he was at heart, doing comic impersonations of himself in print as he later did in the movies. In thus linking oral and written humor, Benchley joined a line of American performers that included George Handel ("Yankee") Hill and Danforth Marble—monologuists who also wrote down impersonations of New England types—as well as Artemus Ward, Bill Nye, Mark Twain, and, more recently, Emily Kimbrough and Cornelia Otis Skinner.

By playing different roles, Benchley could make the monologue a versatile medium of satire. Highet, who finds the monologue of self-exposure an important subspecies of satire, distinguishes between the monologue of conscious and that of unconscious self-exposure. Benchley used both kinds but was more effective with the latter. "The Social Life of the Newt" is unconscious self-exposure, supposedly delivered by Robert Benchley as if from a podium, without one word to indicate that the author is aware of the foolishness he is so solemnly offering as scientific truth. The mask hiding the author remains in place. "This mask is Irony," says Highet, referring to this type of monologue as practiced by Socrates and as used by Swift in *A Modest Proposal*. In the lecture on the newt, "A Talk to a Young Man" (from *The Early Worm*), "Route Nationale 14" (in *From Bed to Worse*), and in several of Benchley's how-to-do-it pieces, the irony is unbroken throughout.

Sometimes Benchley put his monologue in a "frame" in which some background about the speech is provided—the occasion, the physical setting, details about speaker and audience. "The Treasurer's Report," in the volume of the same title, has a framework that includes an "Author's Note" in which Benchley tells how he had happened to improvise this monologue, how he had delivered it in the theater until he was sick of it, and how he is now writing it down for the first time in order to purge himself of it. There are also comments about the speaker, and a few directions for his action, the final "plank" in the frame being *"Exits, bumping into proscenium"* (345). In "Is This the Missing Link?" (from *Pluck and Luck*), the framework is much simpler, consisting only of a subhead, "Bone Fragments Discovered in Weemix and the Problem They Present." Presumably, something like this was the headline on the Sunday feature story that inspired Benchley's parody.

Whether or not he played his role "straight" and feigned unconsciousness of his own humor, Benchley as monologuist often changed masks. To parody tales for or about children, he could play a cantankerous uncle ("Edith"); to satirize the slackness and inefficiency of volunteer workers for charity, he could impersonate a charity worker; to burlesque the pedantry and dogmatism of scholars or scientists, he could impersonate on paper a popularizing lecturer on any subject. Even in writing a piece that was mostly narrative, he would sometimes shift briefly to monologue, as at the end of a disquisition on his difficulties with a banana diet: "And that, kiddikins, is why you must never mention bananas in front of Grandpa if you don't want a good, swift clout across your pretty little mouths."[12] Classroom teachers might also note that many of his essays, whether monologues or not, are more effective when read aloud to a group than when digested silently in solitude.

Benchley was likewise close to the theater when he deviated into dialogue. Occasionally he did this simply because it was a handy way to parody plays. Once in a while he would begin by quoting or summarizing an item from the public press; then he would launch into a dialogue based on an imaginary situation suggested by that item. "Law-Breaking at Its Source" (from *The Treasurer's Report*) was sparked by the appointment of a commission headed by George W. Wickersham to investigate the unenforcement of Prohibition and to report on lawlessness in general. After summarizing this news, Benchley applied the "reduction test" in dialogue form, simplifying the matter to the experience of a little citizen at whose door the entire commission comes knocking. Mr. Welchman, the citizen—who, like Wickersham, is referred to as "Mr. W."—turns the tables and dominates the interview. Through him, Benchley gets off some incidental satire, besides making his main point about the futility of the commission:

Mr. W.: What particular law infractions have you enjoyed most?

Mr. W.: That would be difficult to say, Mr. Wickersham. Sometimes I like one, sometimes another. It all depends on how I happen to be feeling, and on the weather. In summer, for instance, I am rather partial to violating Article 4, Section 6 of the Criminal Code of New York State, but that is because I feel the heat so terribly. In winter I like to devote myself to the Constitutional amendments, although as yet I have never prevented a Negro from voting.

Mr. Baker [Newton D. Baker, former Secretary of War]: They tell me that's a lot of fun.

Benchley did not necessarily pick political topics for treatment in dialogue. "The End of the Season" (from *The Early Worm*), occasioned by a news item about plans to disassemble and move two of the Vanderbilt mansions, is a conversation between two of the Vanderbilt matrons. "Do I Hear Twenty Thousand?" (from *The Benchley Roundup*) sprouted from items in an issue of *Book News* and is an argument involving Swift, Shelley, Tennyson, and other famous authors, and through this debate Benchley ridicules the costly fetishism of rare-book and manuscript collectors as well as the conceit of certain contemporary authors.

Sometimes the dialogue was between Benchley (the "I") and an interlocutor, notably in the sketches about Mr. MacGregor, several of which reappeared in *My Ten Years in a Quandary*. The interlocutor or "straight man" had been used in nondramatic humor before; Mark Twain had created "Mr. Brown" to enliven the account of his travels from San Francisco to New York, and several of Benchley's contemporaries were loosening the genteel tradition with contrasting pairs of comic characters, like Potash and Perlmutter, and Archy and Mehitabel. Benchley probably owed more to the theater and to the actual Mr. MacGregor, his eccentric but likeable factotum on whom the fictional character was based.

However, instead of using either himself or MacGregor merely as straight men, Benchley tended to make the "I" play Mutt to MacGregor's Jeff—the first-person narrator dominates MacGregor but is almost as comical because his confidence exceeds his competence. Thus he accuses MacGregor of losing a locomotive; but, after MacGregor has denied the charge,[13] the conversation somehow digresses and both parties forget what they were talking about. Similarly, the narrator is bothered just as much or more than MacGregor by the Indian rope trick, the Evil Eye, horned owls in his bedroom (no doubt escaped from the same zoo as Thurber's seal), the Cossacks' need for an Ataman, frog farming, climbing the Matterhorn, and the prospect of buying a goat. The narrator is an example of mass-man, or mob-man (or slob-man) like Mutt, Ignatz Mouse, or Jim Kendall in Lardner's "Haircut"; MacGregor is the Little Man, but his tormentor is too inept to be anything but amusing.

Dialogue was only a sometime thing with Benchley, but it became a favorite technique of S. J. Perelman. Typical of Perelman is "Take Two Parts Sand, One Part Girl, and Stir."[14] The narrator, having pondered the arbitrary linkage, in a cosmetics advertisement, of the American Revolution, Hellcat fighter planes and a beach beauty, imagines a colloquy among the sort of advertising men who could hatch such monstrosities of misassociation. As noted earlier, Benchley's movie experience came too late to influence his writing; rather his writing influenced his film productions. Perelman's movie experience began relatively early in his career; however, both humorists exemplify the interrelationship of the modern familiar essay with the stage and with the movies—a topic that needs further probing.

Two other ways in which Benchley helped to revitalize the genteel familiar essay were the roundabout opening and the one-sentence quip or proverb. A device which lends to prose some of the informality of oral delivery is the circuitous opening, in which one begins with a topic that at first seems only distantly related to the main subject, and eases into that subject with the rambling inconsequence of chance conversation. Having tried this sort of opening in *Obiter Dicta*, Benchley used it effectively in one of his earliest pieces done as a free-lance writer, "Call for Mr. Kenworthy!" (in *Of All Things!*).

In the opening paragraph, the narrator comments on how some people wonder what happens to shirt-studs lost at the laundry and to discarded pencil-stubs. Not until the fourth sentence does the author slide into the main topic: "As for me, give me a big, throbbing question like this: 'Who are the people that one hears being paged in hotels? Are they real people or are they decoys?'" Similarly and from the same collection, in "The Community Masque as a Substitute for War" the opening paragraph gives no direct clue to the central subject of the essay:

With War and Licker removed from the list of "What's Going on This Week," how will mankind spend the long summer evenings? Some advocate another war. Others recommend a piece of yeast in a glass of grape-juice. The effect is said to be equally devastating.

Nathaniel Benchley says that this stock opening device was in part "Robert's way of apologizing to his audience—or to himself—for not writing something a little more important. It was advance notice that the piece was going to be fluff, and to hell with it."[15] The narrator in "The Tortures of Week-End Visiting" (from *Of All Things!*) does not get to the subject until the middle of the third paragraph; meanwhile, he has ironically apologized for using the pompous jargon of commentators on more important affairs, such as "the present labor situation." Similarly, in "Mr. Vanity Fair," Benchley consumes three hundred words before mentioning Frank Crowninshield, the subject; and at the end he suggests that the entire sketch is untrustworthy because the subject is his boss.[16]

The roundabout opening had been employed by Holmes and by John Kendrick Bangs; contemporaneously with Benchley's early efforts, Clarence Day, Jr., was giving it his own leisurely satirical touch.[17] In the 1920's Alexander Woollcott made this approach a chatty trademark of his essays on the theater and many other matters.[18] In the use of this device, as in other ways, Benchley was less an originator than a developer and polisher.

Benchley was typical of the revitalizers of high-level humor in wearing the self-satirical mask of a Little Man who interpreted only such elements in great problems as affected his own experience. The humor occasioned by this Little Man's bafflement is not that of insanity but of reason and common-sense in a world so absurd and overpowering as to make the sane man seem the opposite. Benchley often depicts his unheroic hero through dramatic monologue and through dialogue, partly because he was fascinated by the stage and platform and partly because these forms are convenient vehicles of parody. Monologue, dialogue, and the indirect opening were three of the ways in which Benchley helped to rejuvenate the familiar essay. Apart from these primarily structural patterns, Benchley also freshened the language of the essay—another subject.

CHAPTER *8*

Techniques: Through Benchley's Prose
with Gun and Camera

THURBER said that "In all Benchley, a fresh wind stirs in every page."[1] A main source of these zany zephyrs is Benchley's handling of the English language—his quips, his diction, his plays on words, his syntactical acrobatics, and his free association, which ranges from simple digression through non-sequitur to nonsense of a caliber and frequency previously achieved in America only by Gelett Burgess. Striking imagery and sudden irony also whip up whitecaps in the reader's mind, though they seldom send him into gales of laughter.

I *A Part-Time Proverbialist*

According to his son, Benchley never made the quip most often attributed to him, "Let's get out of these wet clothes and into a dry Martini."[2] His basic unit of expression was, in any case, the short essay; nevertheless, he left a fair stock of one-sentence coinages of wisdom and wit. He could give an old line an ironic twist: "Well, in every great cause some few innocent heads must fall," and "A wish without the giver is bare." And he could parody the proverbial style of crackerbox humor as in "Chips from an Old Philosopher."[2]

> How true it is that opposites attract each other. It is Nature's way, I guess, of making her wishes known.
> How true it is that opposites repel each other. I suppose it is Nature's way of making her wishes known.
> There is an old Persian proverb to the effect that we never know *where* we are until we know *how* we are, and that water will run up hill if you push it. A lot of us could take this to heart, I reckon.[3]

One of his salaried writing jobs encouraged him to toss off brief quips—the weekly "Confidential Guide," a department of one- and two-sentence summaries and comments on each current play, which he did for *Life* from 1921 to 1929, in addition to writing the drama reviews. Robert's comments could bite; Nathaniel quotes some snaps at Anne Nichols' *Abie's Irish Rose*— which nonetheless ran for 2,327 performances. Of Avery Hopwood's *Why Men Leave Home*, Benchley said, "Bed-room comedy with a covering of moral." He wrote off *Scandal* by Cosmo Hamilton, as "What no young girl ought to know"; and he dismissed *The Fool* by Channing Pollock with "Showing how Christ, with a little dramatic training, might have handled several modern problems."[4] In wielding the knife-edged quip Benchley was no Dorothy Parker; but he could leave a nasty gash.

II *Strange Wordfellows*

In the realm of vocabulary and diction, Benchley's defense of learning stopped when terms became too abstruse and specialized for the cultivated, common reader. Except to satirize such terms, he rarely used them; and one must leaf through many of his pages to find a sprinkling of words, used seriously, that may have been, at least during the 1920's, on the upper fringe of that reader's zone of comprehension—words such as *adventitious, sobriquet, kleptomaniac, caricature, miasma, ennui, chauvinistic, bucolic,* and *pristine*. On the other hand, he borrowed occasionally from spoken rather than written English. Expressions like *bum* (for incompetent), *hog-wild, stooge, deadpan, nice guy, the hell with, darn* (and *damn*), *mooch, string along, a pretty tough spot, knocking off* (work), and *boost* (to propagandize) would have annoyed Holmes and his imitators; but they helped Benchley to give his generally "correct" writing the informality of conversation and to avoid any danger of stuffiness.

However, Benchley utterly rejected the use of misspellings and malapropisms for their own sakes—a stand-by of cracker-barrel humor. Most Benchley malapropisms occur in parodies and contribute to the feeling that the real source of the absurdity is not the ignorance of the narrator or author who misuses the word, but the style that is being parodied through that misuse: "And so, all through the long, weary summer, Henry Adams sat, head in hand, wondering if Darwin was right. To him the glacial epoch seemed like a yawning chasm between a uniformitarian world and himself."[5] Here "uniformitarian" for Unitarian (or for uniform) occurs in a caption for a movie scenario based on *The Education of Henry Adams;* through free association rather than fact or logic, the malapropism suggests that scenarios and the erudite reminiscences of Adams both have high coefficients of absurdity.

Likewise, whenever the Little Man and mass-man are inept with language, the incompetence usually arises from non-linguistic sources, chiefly anxiety, ignorance, egoism, or a confusion of ideas that strikes in deeper than mere uncertainty with words. After all, most of Benchley's characters reflect their author's university background in having some verbal skill and a fairly large vocabulary.

Once in a while the main cause of a word-jumble is merely the playfulness of the author, as when he turns *thatched hut* into *hutched thatch* and *thatched hutch.*[6] However, anxiety causes the bumbler to blurt out COFFEE, MEGG AND ILK,[7] and ignorance befogs the diction of the amateur music expert in "Music Heavenly Maid" who says Mozart stole from Debusset.[8] Ignorance also handicaps the aggressive narrator who tells Mr. MacGregor that his lack of interest in mountain-climbing shows "a very sub-thyroid attitude of mind."[9] Ignorance of fact and confusion of ideas affect the narrator's reference to "the *Gestalt,* or Rotary-Frictional method."[10] Thurber's Mitty likewise owes his verbal blunders to uncertainties about things and ideas ("Coreopsis has set in."[11]).

Benchley's bumbler also shows his confusions through unnecessary, anti-climactic repetition of words and phrases. Eggs, it seems, are not round but are "more of an 'egg-shape' ";[12] the work done at Silver Lake, according to the Treasurer, "not only fills a very definite need in the community but also fills a very definite need—er—in the community." The Treasurer again runs out of ideas in claiming that he and his cohorts can bring boys into closer touch "with the town in which they live, the country to whose flag they pay allegiance, and to the—ah—(*trailing off*) town in which they live."[13]

Two other forms of word play through which Benchley freshened his style, poked fun at himself, and directly or indirectly satirized other objects were the wild use of proper names, and the pun. Swift's allegorical kingdoms, and such characters of Dickens as Sairy Gamp, Wilkins Micawber, Wemmick, Bumble, Podsnap, and Squeers were larger objects in the mind but were festooned with labels no odder than the beings created by Lewis Carroll, Edward Lear, or Benchley. Robert presented readers with Mr. Ferderber, "Weekins, 1914," Esther Rubric, "Dr. Almer Doctor, Pinks Professor of Obduracy," Darg Gamm, "an old garbler named Leon Nabgratz," and Archlake Turbot, to name a few. Such characters deserved to live at Dormant, Kansas, or at "78 North Creep Street, Noky, Idaho."

In using puns, Benchley could have pointed for precedent to Swift and Thoreau as well as to Holmes, Bangs, and his friends at the Algonquin Hotel in New York City. The pun is merely another way of forcibly joining incongruous contexts. Unexpectedness is probably the most important element in the incongruity; if the reader senses a pun in advance, it is dead. Benchley continually tried to catch his readers unawares with such sudden shifts as "The King, who was still in high dudgeon (the low dudgeons being full of paynims and poor white trash left over from the Fifth, or Crucial, Crusade)...."[14] and the bit about back-seat drivers: "We next come to the class of tonneau-freight who are great believers in what Professor Münsterburg called 'Auto-Suggestion.'"[15] And there is the ill-advised reference to the dentist who was hired to build a bridge for a town because—but one need not go on.[16] Sometimes Benchley turns the low level of pun-wit to advantage. His narrator attempts a bad pun and makes it worse by explanation, as in the parody of Max Eastman's analysis of humor, in which Benchley's man labors over the similarity of "horse" and "hors dé combat."[17]

Scrambled syntax occurs in "The Treasurer's Report," in "From Nine to Five"[18] and in many other pieces, but the most effective of Benchley's syntactics is not mere scrambling but faulty parallelism. As with the pun, Benchley realized that unexpectedness and incongruity were vital. He could say, "In America there are two classes of travel—first class, and with children,"[19] and note that some forms of being unable to say *no* "often lead to electrocution or marriage."[20] On a somewhat larger scale, he could draw up a list of items in which faulty coordination indicated the discontinuity and meaninglessness of the items—and the over-confidence and ineptitude of the statistical, financial, sociological, psychological, or merely promotional experts who did such itemizing. Here (the author implies) is how the sum asked in reparations from Germany was determined:

132, 000 000 000 gold marks
$33, 000 000 000 on a current value basis
$21, 000 000 000 on reparation account plus 12½% yearly tax
on German exports
11, 000 000 000 gold fish
$1.35 amusement tax
866, 000 miles. Diameter of the sun
 2, 000 000 000
27, 000 000 000
31, 000 000 000[21]

For the record, one must show that faulty parallelism of words and phrases was not a monopoly of Benchley and his fellow sophisticates; for example, George Washington Harris had referred to "the spread ove the gospil, an' the measills" in the South by a Northern reporter.[22] Nor was the device confined to the short, primarily humorous sketch; when John Dos Passos in *U. S. A.* apostrophizes the Unknown Soldier about how the army "charted your urine and your intelligence," he can stand for all the novelists who use these techniques. However, false coordination of lists and of whole paragraphs was a specialty of Benchley and his humorous colleagues of the early twenties. To word play and to quirky syntax in general they gave fresh emphasis.

III   *Leaps from Logic*

Benchley could yoke diverse contexts in still other ways. One was anti-climax—the "less-than-to-be-expected ending," as Mody C. Boatright calls it when he finds it in frontier humor.[23] At its best, humorous anti-climax involves an ironic reversal of meaning. After completing his canvass of voters, Benchley's narrator-pollster says to his readers: "We may have had our little differences of opinion, but it has all been good-natured and if we never see any of you again it will be all right with us."[24] In a parody of news releases from explorer-scientists, the reporter-narrator writes:

Last Thursday, for instance, our scoop brought up to the deck of the Reasonably a mess of perfectly dandy things. There were some wee pelagic anemones, all rosy from their ocean dip, little cross-stitch barnacles, several yards of an herbage without a name and which I hope never *does* have a name, a small male watermelon-fish (so-called because it is full of seeds similar to those of a male watermelon), and a safety-razor blade. All these were taken into the ship's laboratory and thrown away.[25]

In both quotations, an anti-climactic reversal of attitude hints at the frivolity of the narrator and of the subject matter. In the second example, the final statement augments, directly as well as indirectly, the satire of the subject matter. A yet different purpose is served by the anti-climax of a piece about the psychologists' view that worrying is good for us. Following a set of "worrying exercises" will make you a new man "and one you will not like."[26] The last clause contains the main implication of the essay.

Nearly all free association *may* be classed as non-sequitur because free association is any use of elements linked in the psyche by connections other than necessarily rational ones. Here, the term "non-sequitur" is applied only to trains of thought wrecked by genuine mistakes of logic on the part of the narrator or by his whimsy or perversity when he is trying to be satirical. (When satire is detected and the author is Benchley, it may be always be assumed that the *author's* satirical intent is conscious.) Faulty parallelism, anti-climax, and irony are arbitrarily excluded from this definition; incompetence or whimsy in regard to thought rather than to mere words or to empirical facts is the most striking quality of what are here labeled "non-sequiturs." For example the inability of the Treasurer to sustain a line of thought makes his Report a mess of non-sequiturs. The bafflement of the bumbler by gadgets leads him into the non-sequitur that they are working together in one great conspiracy to land him in the asylum.

Sometimes the non-sequiturs committed by the narrator throw emphasis on equal or worse fallacies of supposedly more rational people. Individuals who forecast weather by reading goose bones are satirized by a narrator who insists that the behavior of his knee enables him to predict an open winter.[27] (Benchley did have a trick knee, but it didn't help his meteorology.) When a pathologist stated that the age of egotism and of most frequent mistakes was between twenty-five and thirty-five, Benchley, as an ineptly thoughtful Little Man, simply drew the conclusion invited by the statement. Declaring that he had ten more years of the "Danger Period," he added, "I can hardly wait until I'm fifty-five and can be wise, tolerant, conservative and simple."[28] Spoofing the tendency of psychologists (or any other specialists) to seize on simple solutions for complex problems, another narrator swears that he can't work because of his pipe tobacco: "It smells like Saturday, and consequently puts me in a chronic holiday mood."[29]

When Benchley used non-sequiturs as part of parody, he sometimes came close to pure nonsense humor, especially when his target was pretentiousness or complexity. Stressing these qualities could be done by exaggerating the narrator's inability to comprehend, and his attempts would result in a welter of fallacies. Leacock and other pre-*New Yorker* sophisticates tinkered pleasantly with this near-nonsense kind of parody: thus an anonymous bridge expert (the game of bridge was a favorite topic for satire on all levels during the first third of this century) begins a solemnly nonsensical account in *Life* of how to get out of a certain ticklish situation by averring that "Any old cards will do."[30]

Benchley's man stresses his own inability to follow a detective story:

> "It was fairly simple, once we had established the fact that Gilgo could not possibly have been in Chicago with the Matessi gang. O'Rourke and Bleeker we knew were hard up—Greggory told us that—and Maude Marston had been working Dominic to get him to double-cross Vancy. *Now*—on the night when Freebish was seen coming out of Honfnagle's apartment—"
>
> "But it was McCorck who was seen, wasn't it? That was what Teemy reported."
>
> "Teemy reported it because he was afraid that if Clark knew that Noglatz had been playing around with Elsie he would tip off the Gorelli bunch and Szcynocyz would squeal."[31]

This sample is pedestrian in comparison to the satire on "the parlor game of 'Detective'" in which every answer involves a long leap away from logic:

1. A man leaves his home in the morning to go to work. An hour later he is found back in his own bed with a nasty scalp wound. His clothes are folded neatly over a chair. He is unable to talk, but a colored man, who is in bed with him, also with a bad scalp wound, says that he doesn't know who his buddie is, having never seen him before. The police arrest the housekeeper. Why?

Answer. Because she was a notorious counterfeiter.[32]

And when the police can't find John Grunch at a certain address, they are advised to try another (unrelated) address "and ring Dunker's bell." Similarly, C says to A and B, " 'I win! I have two reekers.' There is only one reeker in a 'gummidge' pack. Who won?" The answer is Joe Louis.[33]

IV *The Anatomy of Benchley's Nonsense*

Naturally, the more unpredictable the non-sequitur, the closer it came to nonsense. Nonsensical or "crazy" humor was not new in the exuberant 1920's; Constance Rourke has pointed out the element of nonsense in "Negro" minstrelsy of the 1840's,[34] and nonsense for satirical purposes had sprouted in the *Lark*, edited and written mostly by Gelett Burgess in 1895-1897. Just before World War I, Benchley had been delighted with a Harvard cartoon in which a senior stood at a crossroads, one fork of which was marked "laziness" and the other "industriousness," and asked, "Which way to West Falmouth?"[35] And in 1917 and 1918 the fantastic animals of Oliver Herford were appearing in the *Century* and in *Harper's*.

Four years, almost to a day, after the Armistice, Benchley read "The Treasurer's Report" in a mock revue that also included the first of Lardner's nonsense plays, *The Tridget of Greva*.[36] Another of Benchley's narrators reeled off the chaotic list of figures concerning international finance (quoted near the end of Section II in this chapter) and said, "Then you add them together and subtract the number you first thought of. This leaves 11 and the card you hold in your hand is the seven of diamonds."

In 1924, Edmund Wilson noted the revolution in humor coming about through Joe Cook, Benchley, and "the Algonquin school of humor—the cult of the flat joke, the irrelevant remark, the sophisticated naïveté,"[37] and quoted a Joe Cook joke which was pure nonsense.

However, most nonsense humor turns out to be satire which makes excellent sense. To insist, as does Carolyn Wells, that the nonsense of Lewis Carroll and Edward Lear is no-sense merely because both authors avowed that they took care to avoid ulterior meanings is to fall into the intentional fallacy. Benchley satirized an attempt to read deep meanings into *Alice in Wonderland;* yet he admitted that "It is true that many present-day situations have parallels in the situations of the Alice books, but I like to believe that this is not because Carroll put sense into his nonsense but because the present-day situations are sheer nonsense in themselves."[38] This statement came close to suggesting that meaning was there regardless of the author's intent.

But intent can be only one factor in the reader's evaluation. Reminiscining about the *Lark*, Gelett Burgess wrote: "It contained neither satire, parody, nor comment or criticism of any kind upon contemporary writers." Even so, anyone familiar with the Aubrey Beardsley type of ornate, precious illustration will note that the cartoons, friezes, and curlicues festooning the pages of this little magazine look very much like intentional burlesque of the Beardsley school. The "Purple Cow" quatrain, originally set as it was amid this embroidery, was either a satire on the artificiality in the use of colors by Beardsley and his imitators or it was an awfully pat coincidence.[39]

Nonsense is also the wrong word for most of the material under that heading in *A Subtreasury of American Humor.* The compilers, E. B. White and Katharine S. White, admit that the pieces by Josh Billings and by Don Marquis may not be nonsense. Of the other pieces in the section, the two by S. J. Perelman are parodies; "i'pafm, by Frances Warfield, is a playing around with the tall "s" of the eighteenth century; Lardner's "Sit Still" is a suggestion in narrative that the people who seem to do nothing but sit in hotel lobbies are psychologically if not physically dead; Oliver Herford's verses about animals are coherent exercises in solemn overstatement of the obvious; and so on. Only some of Morris Bishop's "Limericks Long After Lear" and the anonymous limerick about the young belle of old Natchez might be classed as simon-pure nonsense.

The *Subtreasury* does suggest that nonsense elements may be included in fantasy that has an over-all purpose and meaning. A Thurber male sees a unicorn in a fable about how henpecked husbands may turn on their wives. Perelman writes of Philip Forceps, "a young pair of pliers in the employ of John Greenblatt Whittier," but the piece as a whole makes sense as a parody of Sax Rohmer-type thrillers. From Rabelais to the present, the wilder sort of parody has certainly included much fantasy and many touches of pure nonsense. Leacock's *Nonsense Novels* carried to an extreme the distortions in Thackeray's *Novels by Eminent Hands* and Bret Harte's *Condensed Novels*. Most of Lardner's so-called nonsense plays were parodies—of skits for the Ziegfeld Follies, of expressionistic drama from Europe, of Moscow Art Theatre productions, of *Mourning Becomes Electra*. Donald Elder feels that Lardner's plays are parodies only incidentally and that they are even better understood as parts of Ring's lifelong satire on the conversation of the American common man with its pointless stories, its interruptions, irrelevancies, and misunderstandings—in short, its real-life nonsense. "All the time we thought people were making sense, but this is really what they sounded like."[40]

One should add that Lardner's plays rendered what actual stage productions really seemed like in the half-consciousness of the average playgoer: a medley of incoherent fragments. The same approach has been employed by Jonathan Miller, Dudley Moore, and their fellow actors in the "Beyond the Fringe" group: the hilarious hash of gesture and gibberish which they serve up as Shakespeare is their idea of how a Shakespearian production strikes the eye and ear of many in the audience. With both Lardner and the "Fringe," the result is double-edged parody of author and spectator.

Some of Benchley's parody was also rich in "nonsensical" ridicule of both authors and audiences. Fools' gold glittered in "Publicity Playlets," written in 1913 for *Obiter Dicta*. The King pays his Engraver with "a nickel and a cross-town Transfer" and is carried out on the shoulders of his agents, artists, and copywriters, "leaving the Engraver alone on a hydrant":

> *The Sun sets and it begins to Snow and Thunder and Lighten.*
> *The Engraver puts the Nickel in his sock and eats the Transfer.*

Engraver (speaks): "God help the poor Sailors at sea on a Night like this."[41]

The satire is aimed mainly at advertising men and at those who pay them, but indirectly the satire touches all who accept as valid or good the advertising, drama, fiction, song, or essays being mocked. Later, in *Pluck and Luck* (268-73), Benchley mingled clichés and contexts to the point of nonsense in order to emphasize the triteness of one type of sex play.

> *Ronald:* Hello, Mertisse, old girl! Where's your husband?
> *Mertisse:* Oh, Freddie is out whippet-racing.
> *Ronald:* That's fine. Perhaps that will give me a chance to tell you how much I love you.
> *Mertisse:* It will give you a chance all right, but what guarantee have I that you will take it?
> *Ronald:* I'll take that, and a pound of your best coffee, and you can send them, please. I'll take this along with me. (*Kisses her*).

Here, too, the main target is the makers of such pieces, as it is also in "The Blue Sleeve Garter" (from *Pluck and Luck*), a parody of John Galsworthy's economically and politically saturated plays and novels:

> " 'Ware shoals, Melisse!' said Ramsty.
> "Budney, my dear, sheer budney!"
> Trevor bit his lip thoughtfully.
> "You stweem a bit—for you."
> "That will do, Cherry! And please someone take Whang downstairs. He has become intolerable since the Free Trade Club gave him that new leash."
> Whang placed his paws on Lister's spats and said: "Put me out if you will, but remember, I can vote at the next General Election."

Benchley hints that Galsworthy carried his concern for public affairs close enough to nonsense for his work easily to become nonsense should reader or spectator relax his attention slightly.

In Benchley's hands, the hint that a work comes close to nonsense usually results in satire that is good-natured and playful rather than biting or malicious, partly because his wild incongruities are laughable in themselves and partly because they thereby offer an "out" for the reader. People who enjoy *The Good Earth* may ignore Benchley's criticism of Pearl Buck's sentimentalized Chinese peasants and blame the hypothetical audience for carelessly getting the impression that Whang the Gong "was very poor and had only the tops of old Chinese wives to eat."[42]

About the average man's thinking and talking, Benchley could be less good-natured. The unreprinted "Dialectic Hint on How to Win an Argument" includes nonsense humor and an explanation of how this type of nonsense originates in the average man's egotism, ignorance, and pursuit of "one-upmanship" (although Benchley did not use that particular term). People, says Benchley, continually get into arguments over questions about which they know nothing, and each party in a dispute tries to bluff the other. Donning the mask of Little-Man-as-Lout, the author explains that he gets one-up in this kind of argument with "a little set of impressive-sounding events which, so far as I know, have never occurred." He injects them indiscriminately into any discussion, and they are:

1. The Algeciras Incident.
2. The Treaty of Bozen.
3. The Partition of the Engardine.
4. The Gresham-Russell Agreement.
5. The San Marino Fisheries Case.[43]

If he is trapped during an argument over, say, world peace, this white-collar lout can snap, "Why, my dear fellow, how can you say that when you know how the Gresham-Russell Agreement of 1893 worked out?" (Of course, he has thrown in the first date that comes to mind). Or he may counter a statement about American-Mexican relations with " 'How about the Algeciras Incident and the resulting Treaty of Bozen?' (There is no objection to combining any two or more of your references in case you need a mass attack.)" The chances are slight that the listener will admit that he knows as little about these nonexistent events as the speaker does.

Two other plans for injecting nonsense into a conversation may be followed by the returning tourist (or, it is hinted, by the stay-at-home) in order to protect himself from the bores who like to talk about their travels. The first plan, which is based on the fact that few travelers remember more about the places they have visited than the names of one hotel, two points of interest, and perhaps one street, consists of inventing persons and places like Tuna, Louis the Neurotic, and the Man with the Iron Abdomen.[44] The other plan is to let the bores rattle on "and then give unmistakable evidence of not having heard a word they have said." Through either plan, the sane bumbler, be he a hug-the-hearth or an Innocent Abroad, may contribute his share of nonsense to the conversation of the affluent common man.

In addition to satirizing talky-talk, Benchley scored the disjointedness and triviality of the press. Again adopting the oafish role, he said in *After 1903—What?* that "The long stories, concerning international financial scandals and State Department crises, escape me. I am a slave to the oddments in the news." All his eye catches are the fillers and *curiosa* about hundred-striped zebras, wife-murderers, freak accidents, lazy firemen, and weird weather.' As elsewhere, Benchley jabs with twin points: the Little Man is an inattentive reader, but the press really is cluttered with trivia. A similar message concerning this man as a bad receptor and the media as poor conductors is implied in Benchley's satires of popularized science.

Most of Benchley's nonsense yields a solid precipitate of satire, but one does find many drops of sparklingly pure nonsense, based mainly on playful word-association. Frank Sullivan cites Mr. Cassidy in "Safety Second," who fell into a pulp machine "and swashed around until all they had to do was to dry him out and they could have printed the Sunday *Times* on him. In fact, that is just what they did do, and it was one of the best editions of the Sunday *Times* that ever was run off the presses. It had human interest."[45] Perhaps this train of Benchley's thought got switched while he was (as he put it) thumbing through a bit of old snow in the attic or watching Mr. MacGregor leave the office by the door leading into the Rose Bowl.[46]

Just fun and games? Such bits of apparently pure fun as "I look back over Memory Lane, sitting in the fire in front of my pipe" turn into satire when one looks at their contexts. "Memory Lane" was a popular radio serial, and the sentence occurs in a paragraph of soap-opera sentimentality (parodied) in *Pluck and Luck*. The last two sentences of "Horse-Sense Editorial" are obvious word-play, but in context they contribute to the over-all parody of folksy editorials about success: the narrator sees a tree out of line; it isn't playing the game, but he finds out it's a fire-hydrant, and concludes, "Watch out that you aren't a hydrant in a line of trees. Or worse yet, a line of trees in a hydrant."

When the narrator begins a satire on psychoanalysis with "I am a boy of 46, partly white, and stand in my stocking feet,"[47] the interpolated phrase may be read as a quick dig at racial prejudice. In "Significant Results in Second Week of Our Own Straw Vote" the error in geography may be merely a caper, but the sudden shift in mid-passage from one meaning of a word to the other adds to the over-all purpose of the Anti-Bunk campaign: the pollster affirms that "We are on the trail of this trend now and hope to catch up with it any day if we hurry. When last seen, the trend had stopped over in Elkhart, Ill., to set its watch back an hour to Central Standard Time. Or would it be setting its watch *ahead?*"[48] S. J. Perelman, the most dazzling of Benchley's younger contemporaries in making this kind of shift, likewise blends nonsense with satire.[49]

Edmund Wilson compared the nonsense of Joe Cook and of Benchley to Dadaism, a movement which included many items nonsensical in themselves but was, on the whole, a protest against the nonsense and absurdity of the world. This kind of protest is also one of the types of sense in Benchley's nonsense. Benchley's archetypal "crazy" man is not like the fellow whom Albert Camus cites as fishing in a bathtub; on being asked " 'if they were biting,' " he replied, " 'Of course not, you fool, since this is a bathtub'."[50] Camus compared this man to Kafka's hero, who exists in "an indescribable universe in which man allows himself the tormenting luxury of fishing in a bathtub, knowing that nothing will come of it." Benchley's man could use logic quite as illogically,[51] but he retains a clear, if sometimes merely theoretical, belief that basic values do exist and that sometimes it is the world and sometimes merely he himself who is absurd. Meanwhile Robert Benchley, as distinct from his *alter ego*, never changed his belief that law, order, reason, kindness, and compassion were valid and desirable—however ineffectual in specific instances.

The nonsense of later humorists, too, is like mercury—rarely found in the pure state. Some of Thurber's fantastic animals, including most of those in *The Beast in Me,* are truly nonsensical; otherwise, Thurber and Perelman offer much of their alleged nonsense as coherent protest against incoherence and absurdity. The same is true of the controlled nonsense of Edward Albee and of *Mad* magazine; the latter especially is in the tradition of Burgess, Benchley, Thurber, and Perelman, although its doses are more massive and its irreverence is less limited. Whether much of *Mad* is divinest sense or nihilistic chaos is a question probably unresolved by the staff of the magazine, but it and the "absurd" playwrights are heirs of a shrewdly zany tradition in which Benchley played an important part.

CHAPTER 9

Techniques: A Further Venture
into Benchley's Prose

A CARTOON in *Life* (1912) shows a mannish suffragette raising her fist as the cowering male drops his embroidery. An older woman has grabbed her arm and is saying, "You coward, Alice. Would you strike a man?"[1]

The notion of topsy-turviness—of things inverted rather than merely chaotic—is probably universal. Certain primitive peoples have encouraged various individuals to do everything backwards: for example, to go away when told to "Come here," as if these peoples' thinking included consciousness of a world in which every norm might become deviation and the wildest deviations could become normal[2]—and the norm might sometimes be most sharply defined by the deviations.

In Europe, the diabolists—the Marquis de Sade, Charles Baudelaire, Arthur Rimbaud, Friedrich Nietzsche, and Jean Génet—have by their systematic and ironic blasphemy made faith and its concomitant skepticism seem more thoroughgoing than in America. Melville's hanging of the "angel" Billy Budd, Mark Twain's slaughter of innocents in *The Mysterious Stranger,* and O'Neill's ironic glorification of illusion in *The Iceman Cometh* are about as far as Americans have cared to go in reversing the way the universe ought to be. Americans have generally been content to up-end specific, limited contexts, such as war, organized Christianity, democracy, and capitalism.

Examples of limited topsy-turviness in humor are George S. Kaufman's *If Men Played Cards as Women Do* (a far cry from *Lysistrata*), and the attacks by Mark Twain, Ade, and Lardner on the notion that success always goes to the honest, industrious, frugal, and obedient. Mark Twain's paired stories of the bad and good little boys, several of Ade's fables, and Lardner's "Champion" bestow success on the pushy, brash, and ruthless, but they have an irony that shrieks silently, "Things ought not to be this way."[3]

I   *Author* + *Little Man* = *Irony*

Topsy-turviness often teeters on the verge of nonsense, but it is too neat to be nonsense. Rather, such inversion is verbal irony —a stating of the opposite of what one really means. This statement may be a single sentence, as in Benchley's reference to a Mr. Strickland as "a man of science, and understanding the spirit of my research."[4] Actually, Mr. Strickland's only claim to fame is that he played the piano for 122½ hours without a stop, and Benchley carefully let slip that his own "research" consisted of writing this humorous piece.

Verbal irony may also be practiced, however, on the scale of paragraphs, subsections, and whole articles or essays. Most of Benchley's many "how" pieces are actually instructions on how *not* to accomplish the end in question. One should read carefully "How to Avoid Colds," "How to Understand Music," and "How One Woman Kept the Budget from the Door," and then do the opposite of what Benchley recommends.[5] The reader will be better prepared for Benchley's "anti-instruction" if he has read Franklin's "Rules by Which a Great Empire May Be Reduced to a Small One."[6]

Irony of understatement and of overstatement may be conveniently if not absolutely distinguished from mere statements of the exact opposite of one's real meaning. Benchley enjoyed making ponderous understatements, in the *Punch manner,* of the perfectly obvious. In parodying Amy Lowell's life of Keats, Benchley causes the pedant-as-boob to reprint a wretched poem entitled "Lines on Opening a Letter and Finding Sand in It" (actually part of the Benchley canon); the pedantic persona characterizes this abortion as "not perfect."[7] A description of the Little Man's efforts to perform calisthenics includes, "You can run up and down stairs in a twenty-story building if you like, but people who do that are always dropping dead, and that's no fun either."[8] In a commentary on the lost art of cursing, the author quotes a triple-decker malediction hurled at the

Greek statesman Venizelos and then adds, "It was obvious that the patriot was taking sides in the election, or at any rate, had leanings."[9]

Overstatement—the least interesting technique of frontier tall-tale tellers and a standby of tired humorists in general—sometimes sprang with new life from Benchley's typewriter. The final example listed in "Phobias" is "optophobia, or the dread of opening the eyes for fear of what they will see.."[10] Benchley's exagerated stress of his troubles with gadgets and machinery has fooled some critics into thinking him totally helpless instead of merely slower and more awkward than average when opening cans or closing a suitcase:

> In putting on a ribbon I lose myself entirely, and invariably end up completely festooned like Laocoön, ripping and tearing madly with inkstained fingers at a ribbon which long before I had rendered useless. . . the best that I can do is break the typewriter . . . But really . . . after all . . . youxxxxx you xxxxxxxxxxxx take that xxxxxxxxxxxx and *that* xxxxxxxxxxxx.[11]

But the author got the essay written despite the Little Man's difficulties.

In his use of all three brands of verbal irony, Benchley's purpose is more than mere entertainment; he is trying, like Thoreau, to wake up his readers. Unlike his fellow Yankee, however, he is less apt to "brag as lustily as chanticleer" than to belittle himself in mock-heroic fashion (which Thoreau could do too). Nor does he owe much to the frontier brag; his main debt is to Joe Jackson, Joe Cook, and other portrayers of the forlorn tramp on stage and on silent screen. To their desperate clowning Benchley added a whimsical prose style and a white collar.

II *Benchley's Imagery and What It Tells Us*

Extended discussion of Benchley's imagery is not possible here, but certain image clusters may be noted which convey the uniqueness of his humor and also reveal patterns of thought and feeling characteristic of his fellow humorists. Withdrawal and aggression form the patterns in two recurring clusters; terror and violence, a third.

Benchley's feelings of withdrawal and of aggression may be phases of the search for an image of the self that would bring inner harmony and outer integration with family and society. This search for self preoccupied Jay Gatsby, Nick Adams, Eugene Gant, and Danny O'Neill—to name only a few partial surrogates for their authors. One has no right to say that Benchley's problem cost him less pain than that of say, Thomas Wolfe; but judged by the external facts of Benchley's life, he felt less alienated from self and from society than some of the famous fictioneers. With little apparent difficulty he conformed to the basic Judeo-Christian ethic and, like H. L. Mencken, usually obeyed "all laws that are physiologically obeyable."[12] Shortly after his marriage, Benchley wrote in his diary, "I have found in my Wife a joy that I had never dreamed of. I still have to find myself";[13] but he later wrote—admittedly for public consumption—that he had given up this search.[14] Whatever its degree of urgency, his quest for identity was refracted in short pieces featuring an author-surrogate that could serve as basis for much comedy about small matters and for some implications about large ones—but could occasion little pathos and no tragedy.

Nevertheless, withdrawal and aggresion were two ways in which Benchley registered through his bumbler some tension in his desire for inner harmony and outer integration. Through withdrawal the Little Man might admit defeat by a specific problem; one recourse of this character in defeat is simply to lie down or to hole up. In *No Poems* the prospect of carrying his luggage or of asking a porter to carry it for him causes the Benchley persona to figure that "Perhaps it would be better yet not to go anywhere, and just sit in my room."[15] His frustration by taxis leads him to consider not using cabs at all, and the impracticality of parcel-post regulations and the discourtesy of postal clerks finally drive him away from the window, "sobbing."

These defeats are inflicted by external forces; some other problems are largely self-generated. In "Mind's Eye Trouble" a sense of inadequacy (actually part of the mask through which the author delivers shrewd comments on readers and reading) makes him think, "Perhaps I had just better give up reading entirely. But then what else is there to do?"[16] The whistles, yells, honks, and bangs in the modern city are symbolized by the tootling of a blind clarinetist under his window, and the conflict of conscience arising from his desire to silence this noise causes the Little Man to shut all the windows and get under the bed "to sulk."[17]

Optical illusions discussed by scientists (and advertisers) arouse in him the fear that if he can't believe his own eyes, he can't believe anything at all. "The whole thing becomes frightening once you start to think of it. So don't think of it." Typically, Benchley presents a serious problem—in this case, the epistemological one of the nature of perception—on a farcical level, but from behind his mask of anxiety he jabs in passing at other follies—here, at worn-out proverbs, oversimplified feature articles, and especially militarism: a regiment of marching soldiers turns out to be "a crowd of rather ungainly sheep, walking on their hind legs."[18] Likewise, Thurber works his satire of trashy melodrama and of domineering wives into the withdrawal fantasies of Walter Mitty, and Perelman strikes a blow for privacy by suggesting that unrestrained use of candid cameras may drive even the honest citizen into—well, into seclusion: "The Bonnie Brae is not a booby-hatch in the old-fashioned sense."[19]

Instead of withdrawing, the Little Man of White, Thurber, Perelman, and Benchley sometimes lashes back, but with varying effectiveness. Benchley's man in *No Poems*, dreams of getting a group of kids to fire back at adults the silly questions they ask them until "the grown-ups were down on the floor kicking and screaming."[20] His failure to answer the botanical questions on placards in Central Park rouses him to strike back (in his mind) with placards of his own asking, "How much macadam would it take to fill up this hole, and why the hell isn't it done?" and "Who killed Arnold Rothstein?"[21] He tells a pesky insurance salesman that he wants insurance against insurance salesmen (but loses that round because the salesman promptly writes him such a policy).[22] He wonders why clerks in tourist bureaus never blackjack some of their oafish customers.[23] He warns all who jumble the pages in the Sunday news—especially his family— that "I am going to stand just so much more of this thing and then away *some*body goes to the police station."[24] He smashes his typewriter, and he declares war on pigeons; but the hostility which is often futile and destructive can be channeled constructively into criticisms of theater audiences and sensible recommendations for the improvement of taxi service.[25]

But Benchley's bumblers tend, on the whole, to be less extreme and more constructive in their aggressions than Thurber's neurotics. For example, in "Ladies' Wild" by Benchley and "Everything Is Wild" by Thurber,[26] both males hate any variation from orthodox poker; but Benchley's man merely feels hurt when left out of the ladies' game, insists on sitting in, loses heavily, and winds up laughing ruefully at himself for trying to play the role of the Big Newspaperman who knows poker. Thurber's man (who is so full of hostility anyway that "he never liked anybody he hadn't met before") takes active revenge by making up wild variations of his own, wins heavily, augments the already considerable tension between him and his wife, and decides that "He had a swell time after all." The hostility of Thurber's little men creates part of the dramatic tension that has made Thurber's best work more popular than Benchley's. Perhaps other humorists could find irony in the thought that Benchley's little men tend to be nicer guys and that his work is less well known than Thurber's.

III   "What About A Good, Loud Scream?"

Sometimes the aggressiveness in Benchley's humor is revealed in images of death, violence, and terror. At Phillips Exeter, he wrote a composition on how to embalm a corpse,[27] but his interest in the macabre was pretty well channeled later in the service of his moral zeal (not counting the time he took a punch at a bird). His hostility quotient was probably about normal, but the pratfall and Punch-and-Judy elements in stage humor, the home-grown violence of humor during the frontier period, and the international violence during which his career began and ended may all have augmented the hostilities of Benchley's bumbler.

In any case, this narrator hatched a scheme for poisoning playgoers who clap at the wrong places; and when a woman laughed at the off-stage shot in *The Wild Duck*, he "had her killed."[28] To be used on football fans who shout suggestions to the quarterback, Benchley's fan announced the sale of "a special folding pocket dagger this season (with sheepskin case, $7.00). It will go through any fur coat, no matter how heavy, and will inflict a dangerous if not fatal wound."[29] Benchley did not think it was funny to see anyone slip on a banana peel,[30] but in the realm of fantasy he made humor out of a man's having to take three children from Philadelphia to Boston on a hot day. At Hartford he had only two; at Worcester, one; and he reached Boston alone.[31] And Mr. Peters, one of Benchley's rare third-person protagonists, poisons an oafish companion because he made him "conspicuous in a public place."[32]

One function of macabre imagery in Benchley's work is to make moral judgments less severe and more comic by removing them to the realm of fantasy. The second use is to reinforce the humorist's caricature of himself as comic protagonist. The lethal ways of the traveler with his children and the over-reaction of a football fan to whoever dares to advise him about the plays ("If you did do this, however, you are not alive today—not if the man next to you was I.") are part of the humorist's self-caricature, as is the smashing of the typewriter by the frustrated writer.

A third function appears in parody: imagery of terror forms a logical part of any parody of literary or theatrical violence. "Family Life in America," "Editha's Christmas Burglar," "Happy Childhood Tales," "Drama Cleansing and Pressing," and "Fascinating Crimes"[33] parody, respectively, the realistic novel, the sentimentalizing of criminals in a children's story, the macabre fairy tale, three kinds of sex drama, and accounts of famous crimes written by raconteurs like Edmund Pearson and Alexander Woollcott. Published in 1921, within a year after Sinclair Lewis' *Main Street,* Sherwood Anderson's *Poor White,* and Zona Gale's *Miss Lulu Bett* had hit the bookstalls (and had been reviewed by Benchley in the New York *World*), "Family Life in America" is so exaggerated in its combining of violence with minute, homely detail as to seem more like a burlesque, in the manner of Thurber's "Bateman Comes Home," of the yet unwritten novels of Faulkner or of Erskine Caldwell. Such exaggeration suggests more gusto than was required merely for parody. Benchley's idyll ends:

> In the dining room of the Twillys' house everything was very quiet. Even the vinegar cruet which was covered with fly-specks. Grandma Twilly lay with her head in the baked potatoes, poisoned by Mabel, who, in her turn, had been poisoned by her husband and sprawled in an odd posture over the china-closet.

Wilbur and his sister Bernice had just finished choking each other to death and between them completely covered the carpet in that corner of the room where the worn spot showed the bare boards beneath, like ribs on a chicken carcass.[34]

Only the baby survived. She had a mean face and had great spillings of Imperial Granum down her bib. As she looked about her at her family, a great hate surged through her tiny body and her eyes snapped viciously. She wanted to get down from her high-chair and show them all how much she hated them.

Bernice's husband, the man who came after the waste paper, staggered into the room. The tips were off both his shoe-lacings. The baby experienced a voluptuous sense of futility at the sight of the tipless lacings and leered suggestively at her uncle-in-law.

"We must get the roof fixed," said the man, very quietly. "It lets the sun in."[35]

The macabre in Benchley's work has yet a fourth function: to burlesque a society warped by war and ridden with crime. As a remedy for postwar boredom, "Some advocate another war";[36] happily, most prefer the community masque. Self-satire, as well as social satire, is included in "Johnny-on-the-spot" in which Benchley pretends he is one of the Little Men who saunter through life and the news photos oblivious to the fall of dynasties and the collapse of cities—"provided we do not get hit by stray bullets."[37] One reason the narrator can't toddle along from a party is that "Somebody might do card tricks, or shoot somebody else."[38] In the same volume, he remarks: "When you come to think of it, the wonder is not that there are so many jammed automobile fenders, bad motion pictures, sore throats, divorces and wars, but that there aren't *more* of them. We are living in a world that is shot through with luck, that's all."[39]

Less obviously but no less definitely functional are the grisly morsels that Benchley seems to have thrown in mainly for contrast with lighter themes. He begins one piece in *No Poems* with "Having nothing to worry me right now (except a slight dropping away of bits of the base of my brain, which any good doctor can fix up in no time) I am beginning to fret about children's games" (192). The work really is mainly about children's games, and the opening is an indirect way of maintaining the author's pose that he was a light-minded funnyman who ignored basic phenomena like time, deterioration, and death in order to write trivia. Nevertheless, these great subjects are there by implication whenever Benchley uses gallows-humor in a strategic spot. Apart from the occasions when he lashed out directly against remediable violence and injustice, he preferred to touch lightly both upon social grievances and upon man's irremediable doom. The contrasts of trivia and grimness would be oppressive if the author had not made them so incongruous that the reader may find release in laughter.

The relative lightness and brevity of Benchley's gallows-humor may be seen more readily if contrasted with the *grotesquerie* of certain Europeans—the drawings of Kathe Köllwitz and George Grosz, for example, or the *Galgenlieder* (*Songs from the Gallows*) of Christian Morgenstern. One of Morgenstern's lyrics depicts "a knee wandering through the world on its own, since the man to whom it once belonged was destroyed all around it in some war."[40] Benchley seldom pushed his anger about war or his awareness of death at the reader; he preferred the pinprick and the fleeting twist of the lip. A single-sentence fragment about war in *The Treasurer's Report*—"just as surely as if he had died in the trenches"—is worked into a series of fragments parodying the banquet speeches given in the old Waldorf and is enough to suggest that hypocrisy about war was part of the general hypocrisy and sentimentalism of such orations.[41]

The following excerpts are equally quick side-glances at the abyss. They occur, respectively, in pieces about Christmas legends, books suitable for Christmas gifts, Turkish baths, the scientific attitude toward eating, the "insight" of psychoanalysts, scientific experiments with liquor, and the alleged pleasures of solitary communion with nature:

> And so it happened that late on Christmas Day the King rolled over and, finding his head where it had bounced under the bed, replaced it on one shoulder and rubbed his eyes, which he found in the pocket of his waistcoat.[42]

> The surest way to get rid of pests is to fumigate with hydrocyanic acid in an airtight compartment, but this is a dangerous procedure which has resulted in a loss of human life. [Why "but"?][43]

> I can imagine no lower point of self-esteem than to find yourself one day the worst-looking exhibit in a Turkish bath. They

should keep a pistol handy for just such cases. And you might shoot a couple of others while you are at it. It would save them all that bother of lacing up their shoes again.[44]

I suppose that it's all right to carry on that way if you are a biologist, but sooner or later that kind of life gets you and you break up into millions of little "taste-buds" and blow out the window.[45]

Now it turns out that, when I lie down to go to sleep, my throat closes up and I stop breathing. This idiosyncrasy brings me, like a flash, out of bed and onto my feet in the middle of the floor, looking for the electric light.[46]

The only cure for a real hangover is death.[47]

Maybe that's the top of your head flying off—or was it just a gull going by? Suppose it were a gull *with* the top of your head! What about a good, loud scream?[48]

Mark Twain, who piled the bodies high at the end of *A Conecticut Yankee;* Ring Lardner, whose hotel sitters are examples of death in life; Thurber, whose Mr. Kinstrey went madder about the whip-poor-will (and about some other things) than Benchley ever did about pigeons and bluejays; Perelman, who can end a humorous piece with the poisoning of a hall full of diners[49]—these writers, too, have written American choreography for the *danse macabre* that is part of some humor in all ages and has whirled prominently through comic literature during a half-century of total war and mass insecurity.

Stressing the somber element in Benchley's humor is perhaps the wrong way to close a discussion of his techniques. He and his peers of the Algonquin, *Life,* and *The New Yorker* were, after all, only a little more pessimistic and a little more given to macabre imagery than were such crackerbox philosophers as Kin Hubbard, Ed Howe, and Will Rogers. To agree with Thurber, White, and many other theorists that melancholy is basic in humor is merely to note that no first-rate humorists are Pollyannas. "Nothing dont mean anything,"[50] wrote Will Rogers; but his skepticism did not prevent him from being a great humanitarian, a vigorous supporter of the New Deal, and a smiling philosopher more often than a dark one. The irony, pessimism, and gallows-humor that tinged many of Benchley's most playful pieces awaits study by a depth psychologist, but these elements in his humor were only a few of those through which this monologuist-in-print held his "audience"—and that audience smiled, chuckled, or quivered with laughter more often than it cried.

CHAPTER 10

The Benchley Mark

B ENCHLEY influenced the humor of his time as speaker, writer, movie-maker, and individual. As a professional humorist he brought new verve and sophistication to genteel humor and stimulated others to do likewise. As a person he commanded respect and inspired friendship among his literary colleagues to an extent few writers have done.

I *A Writer's Reputation and How It Grew*

Benchley, as a humorist, scored first through his improvised oral monologues. Among the impersonations of a politician and of a traveler that he performed while still a Harvard under-graduate was "Through the Alimentary Canal with Gun and Camera" which inspired George S. Chappell to write his best and most enduring piece of humor.[1] The dinner following the Harvard-Yale game of 1914 was enlivened when Benchley, with some help from a Chinese whom he got to pose as an expert on Oriental football, delivered a speech which earned him the accolade, "the greatest humorist of all time at Harvard"[2]—a premature but prophetic judgment that did no injustice to James Russell Lowell and Oliver Wendell Holmes.

As a writer, Benchley was in demand before he had ever been paid for a line. He was still a senior at Harvard when the editor of the Boston *Journal* asked him to write a daily humorous column for that paper.[3] Ironically, Robert had difficulty breaking into print, but the first humorous piece he published for pay as a free-lance writer in *Vanity Fair* (1914) drew a letter to the editor from Rupert Hughes saying, "whoever this Robert C. Benchley is, let us have more of him."[4]

More came, and observers of the literary scene realized that a new brand of humor was in the making. In 1915, as has been stated, literary agent Paul Reynolds asked for the chance to market Benchley's humor. Burton Rascoe, reviewing *Of All Things!* and volumes by Frank Moore Colby, Clarence Day, Jr., Simeon Strunksy, Christopher Morley, and Max Beerbohm, made special mention of Benchley's use of the Declaration of Independence as a preface. Roscoe added: "For I hold these truths to be self-evident: that in the field of essay writing contemporary Americans are incomparably superior to the modern Englishman."[5] In effect, Rascoe felt that American humorists were outpunching *Punch.*

In 1923 a reviewer for the New York *Times* felt that American writers had not yet matched Beerbohm, Shaw, and Anatole France in irony and satire. This country was on the way, but "For the time being we must content ourselves with George Ade, Finley Peter Dunne, Don Marquis, Robert C. Benchley, F. P. A., and men of that more popular stamp. We are still a young nation; we are still quite ignorant of super-sophistication."[6] By that last term, the reviewer evidently meant irony of understatement applied to high-level subject matter, but he praised the "exaggeration par excellence" and the "mock gravity" of Benchley. Writing of Benchley's first book, E. L. Pearson felt that the dominance of crackerbox humor lay in the past and that Benchley might soon "take the place that Artemus Ward, Josh Billings, George Ade, and F. P. Dunne had held in their own days."[7]

Gilbert Seldes and Edmund Wilson especially enjoyed the satire of business and businessmen in *Of All Things!*[8] and Wilson (who was managing editor of *Vanity Fair* for a short while after Benchley had resigned) found Benchley "more urbane than Leacock" but wished he were "more savage" and more comprehensive in his social satire, like Sinclair Lewis, and that he would cling less to "the pleasant nonsense of the Harvard Lampoon"—a criticism that paralleled Benchley's self-recriminations for not writing more solid stuff. In reviewing *Love Conquers All,* Wilson repeated his criticism; but he considered this book, Benchley's second collection, to be "a devastating book" and hailed its author as "the Scarsdale Aristotle."[9]

Reviews of Benchley's later books also implied recognition of his relatively high-brow approach and of the vitality he brought to it. John Farrar, who called him "the great philosopher in short pants ... the Santayana of the Algonquin, the Plato of Broadway," recommended him "primarily as a philosopher." Discussing *After 1903—What?*, William Rose Benét observed that Benchley's books "make more sense than Gertrude Stein"— a pointless comparison had it been made with a crackerbox oracle like Will Rogers—and stressed Benchley's nonsense and spontaneity: "The man is spontaneously cuckoo."[10]

Some of Robert's fellow humorists were even sharper in seeing the sense in Benchley's nonsense. Frank Sullivan wrote that "Every sentence the reader traversed with him was apt to become an adventure" but not an irresponsible one: "His lance pierced more shams than all the preachments of the indignation boys and do-gooders. He was the sanest of men and saw things clearly. He had humility, honesty and integrity." Thurber stated that "In all his books, you find him ducking swiftly, looking closely, writing sharply." Writing of Perelman, Dorothy Parker implied that he had "a disciplined eye and a wild mind" as well as the courage to be critical; in these qualities, she felt, Benchley "was probably nearest to Perelman."[11]

In a foreword to Perelman's *Strictly from Hunger*, Benchley suggested that the younger writer was his heir apparent as a maker of nonsense: "Perelman took over the *dementia praecox* field." And Perelman dedicated *The Best of S. J. Perelman* to Benchley. Another significant inscription is Groucho Marx's dedication of *Groucho and Me*: "To Those Six Masters Without Whose Wise and Witty Words My Life Would Have Been Even Duller: Robert Benchley, George S. Kaufman, Ring Lardner, S. J. Perelman, James Thurber, E. B. White." This tribute lends plausibility to a chain of influence suggested by Martin Esslin: "Ring Lardner's nonsense is closely related to the nonsense monologues of Robert Benchley. Another among the large number of brilliant American practitioners of nonsense prose is S. J. Perelman, who was responsible for some of the best dialogue in the Marx Brothers films and who has therefore directly influenced the Theatre of the Absurd."[12]

Benchley's popularity could not match that of Will Rogers with his hundred million or more readers, but the syndicated column that Benchley wrote three times a week in the early 1930's went to sixteen mass-circulation newspapers, including the New York *Daily News*, the Boston *Globe*, the Washington,

D.C. *Times*, and the Cleveland *Plain Dealer*.[13] Four volumes of his selected pieces have gone on living and by the spring of 1963 had each sold an average of 46,000 copies. Not phenomenal sales, but all four works continue to sell,[14] mostly, one suspects, to suburbanites with a college or university orientation. Many more readers, of course, have been reached by separate pieces scattered in anthologies.

II *The Round Table*

During his career, Robert moved through a series of constantly changing and loosely interrelated groups of writers and journalists who, like himself, were adding more meat as well as more sauce to American humor. On the *Lampoon,* he worked with Frederick Lewis Allen, E. L. McKinney, Gluyas Williams, and other university wits whose production of humor did not cease with their graduation. In two stints with the New York *Tribune* he worked under Franklin P. Adams and with Arthur Folwell, Heywood Broun, and George S. Kaufman. At *Vanity Fair,* Benchley worked with Dorothy Parker and Robert E. Sherwood; at *Life,* with Sherwood, Charles Dana Gibson, Thomas L. Masson, E. S. Martin, George S. Chappell, Marc Connelly, and others. Many of these writers knew one another through several connections, but few were conscious imitators of any man's style, living or dead.

The influence of the Algonquin Round Table on Benchley and on American humor in general is therefore hard to determine. Margaret Case Harriman says of the group: "Its influence on American literature, drama, and humor was acute, untiring and permanent." Dorothy Parker, writing many years later, has claimed that people "romanticize" the group and that "The round table was just a lot of people telling jokes and telling each other how good they were."[15] Margaret Case Harriman sensibly says, "None of these men ever said to any other, 'Hey! Let us start a regular lunch-group at the Algonquin and call it the Round Table'."[16] Apparently, Broadway literati began to eat there regularly because the location was handy and they liked the pastry. In 1919, Benchley, Sherwood, and Miss Parker got into the habit of lunching there, and so, as time went on, did Adams, Broun, Kaufman, Connelly, Harold Ross, Alexander

Woollcott, Laurence Stallings, Edna Ferber, Ina Claire, Margalo Gillmore, and other high-powered personalities from nearby newspapers, magazines, and theaters. At first, they ate singly or in small groups, but after they began to cluster, manager Frank Case moved them to a large round table.

People came and went from the Round Table over the years, but there is no doubt that some cohesiveness and a great deal of mutual stimulation characterized the group as a whole during the period between two wars. One unifying force was love of wit and of showing off wit to each other. (Peggy Wood, an actress, rose one day, remarked "Well, back to the mimes," and admitted later that she had thought of the pun the night before and could hardly wait to utter it at the Table.[17]) Other forces for cohesion were respect for hard work and good workmanship, debunking of phoniness (including their own), and active social conscience which stood out in contrast to the widespread moral apathy of the 1920's: "The entire Round Table rose up in arms to protest the arrest and conviction of Sacco and Vanzetti."[18] Within a very few years, accounts in the press of the group's jokes and quarrels had surrounded it with a mist of legend but had also generated among the members another unifying force: collective self-consciousness of their position as an unofficial but real social unit and as a moot court of letters.[19]

Mutual influences among the group were tangibly embodied in several theatrical projects. John Peter Toohey introduced George S. Kaufman to a producer who commissioned Kaufman and Marc Connelly to write a play about a character featured in Franklin P. Adams's column; the result was *Dulcy* (1921), the first success for both playwrights. Two satirical revues were prepared and acted by the Vicious Circle, and less ambitious entertainments were improvised by the Round Tablers in the studio of Neysa McMein.

One direct, important, and—from a literary point of view—not wholly good influence of the Table on Benchley came through these two satirical shows. One of the two enduring pieces in them was "The Treasurer's Report" (the other was Lardner's *The Tridget of Greva*[20]). As a result of this improvisation, "My life changed its course."[21] Benchley's performance got him an unsought-for spot to deliver the piece in a Broadway show. An assignment to film the "Report" followed in 1928, and Benchley, from that time on, was interested in the Hollywood money that gradually lured him altogether from writing.

III   *The New Yorker*

The Round Table became a center of wit and ideas in 1919; *The New Yorker* began publication in 1925. Before he began sitting in at the Algonquin, Harold Ross may have had the idea for a humorous weekly that would combine the smartness of the metropolis with the informality of a small-town newspaper. But Ross got some specific ideas, as well as much moral support, from the Algonquin cluster. For example, Woollcott, Broun, Connelly, Kaufman, Stallings, Miss Parker, and Edna Ferber were on the original board of nominally "Advisory Editors," and Toohey suggested the title for the new magazine.[22] More importantly, most of the Round Table members had already written considerable humor in newspaper or magazine columns and as essays or articles. Even without considering established humorists who had no affiliation with the Round Table, such as Day, Mencken, Nathan, and Marquis,[23] one sees that a full-fledged milieu of smart, informal metropolitan humor existed before the first *New Yorker* rolled off the presses on February 21, 1925.[24]

This point deserves emphasis because of the persistent notion that modern American humor sprang full-blown into being with Ross's magazine, a notion overly supported by the fact that Ross got little specific help from most of the Algonquin crew during the critical first year of the new periodical. The board of "Advisory Editors" was collected just to please backer Raoul Fleischmann who wanted well-known names in the magazine; its services as a board were nil.[25] Thurber says that the Round Table "and its fringes" took Ross's project lightly and helped him out rather little and rather late.[26] Dorothy Parker submitted only one prose piece and two poems in 1925, and her book reviews signed "Constant Reader" did not begin until October, 1927. Ten months elapsed before Benchley's first piece appeared in the magazine, on December 19, 1925; and a year went by before Gluyas Williams, illustrator of Benchley's Little Man, contributed to Ross's periodical.

However, part of the debt owed by Ross to Benchley and his milieu is traceable. In two respects, the general appearance and

format of *The New Yorker* in 1925 somewhat resembled that
of *Vanity Fair*. First, both magazines displayed a wonderland
of advertisements, especially for clothing and for such luxury
items as perfume, jewelry, and golf equipment. Secondly, the
frequency in *The New Yorker* of drawings by Williams, Rea
Irvin, and several other artists who had also contributed to
Vanity Fair lent further similarity to both periodicals. *Life*,
too, shared some of these illustrators and some of that similarity. More specifically, *The New Yorker* borrowed the title
of Benchley's first book, *Of All Things!* as the standing head
for a department of quips by Howard Brubaker, and it set up
a listing of current plays under "What's Going On" with a
caption pithily summarizing each attraction. This department
resembled the "Confidential Guide" in *Life* as written (though
not originated) by Benchley.

Aside from Ross, the shapers of what is loosely called *The
New Yorker* style were two young newspapermen, E. B. White
and James Thurber whom Ross hired in 1926 and 1927, respectively. They developed, chiefly in the "Talk of the Town"
section, the reputation of the magazine for understatement,
condensed chattiness, and sly whimsy. White and Thurber had
grown up as writers in the tradition of metropolitan humor
represented by Franklin P. Adams (who once filled a whole
column of "The Conning Tower" with a contribution by the
then unknown Thurber[27]) and by Marquis, Colby, Day, Benchley,
Broun, Mencken, and Nathan.

Moreover, at first lacking the assistance of such luminaries as
these, *The New Yorker* got off to a poor start. As Thurber says,
"Its early issues went in for a frivolous and curiously small-
town kind of joke, an almost subcollegiate flippancy, and a
self-conscious, intramural urbanality."[28] The immense improvement during the first ten years came partly through the capacity
for professional growth of Ross, White, and Thurber, partly
through belated but frequent contributions from established
talent like Benchley, Lardner, Miss Parker, Arthur Kober, Day,
and Broun, and partly through the offerings by younger up-
comers like Frank Sullivan, S. J. Perelman, Wolcott Gibbs,
Ogden Nash, Will Cuppy, and Sally Benson.[29]

Writers in all three categories admired Benchley and studied
his writing. In "The Incomparable Mr. Benchley," Thurber indi-

cates that "I read and admired everything he ever wrote" and that "Benchley beat me to a lot of things, including the Algonquin pigeons and the *Eclaireur* of Nice, whose murky cuts he said were 'presumably etched on pieces of bread.' His day dreamer, cool and witty on the witness stand (1935) and in heroic peril (1932), antedated a little old day dreamer of my own named Mitty."[30]

Thurber (five years younger than Benchley) and White (ten years younger) admitted that they may have merely imitated Benchley for some time, and Thurber has quoted White's statement that "The day Ross told me Benchley had praised something I had written was one of the big days of the twenties for me."[31] Tributes quoted by Thurber from Gibbs, Sullivan, and Donald Ogden Stewart also testify to Benchley's standing among humorists.

After the first year of *The New Yorker*, Benchley's direct help in improving the magazine was probably as strong as that of any other one writer except White and Thurber. Benchley began writing "The Wayward Press" department in 1927, took over as drama critic for the magazine in 1929, and contributed freelance pieces from 1926 on. Benchley is Exhibit A in the evidence that where the development of smart, urbane humor featuring the Little Man is concerned, *The New Yorker* represented not a beginning but a climax.

IV *From Writing to Films*

At a party given around 1939, Robert burst out in a manner unusual for so kind and tactful a man. Pointing at Robert E. Sherwood, who had just received the second of his three Pulitzer prizes for playwriting, Benchley said, "He's looking at me and thinking of how he knew me when I was going to be a great writer.... And he's thinking *now* look at what I am."[32] By that date Benchley was almost a full-time actor and writer for Metro-Goldwyn-Mayer, although during the next year he shifted to Paramount.

Millions of people who never read Benchley must have seen him as Little Man on the screen;[33] however, it cannot be shown clearly, as has been noted, that his movie work exercised any influence one way or another on his sketches and essays. The gradual shift from writing to films came mainly because movie-making was fun, easy, and lucrative—Nathaniel Benchley says that Robert was "physically unable to save money"—and because other writing was hard and never so lucrative as working in pictures. The end of Benchley's career as a writer may be dated with the appearance in 1938 of *After 1903—What?*, his last original collection. During the next year the party occurred at which he voiced his hidden discontent.

V A *Major-Minor American Humorist*

The urge to write may have weakened, but not Benchley's satirical outlook. Just before his last, hurried trip to the hospital, he was reading an essay, "Am I Thinking?" by James Harvey Robinson, and he wrote in the margin, "NO (and supposing you were?)."[34] His death from a cerebral hemhorrhage at age fifty-six left battalions of friends and acquaintances feeling much as Benchley had felt when an actor he admired was killed in an accident: "There was really no sense in that, Lord, and you know it as well as I do."[35]

Long before his death Benchley had become (the label would have amused him) at least a major-minor American humorist. Beginning as a casual exploiter of collegiate topics for the amusement of fellow-students and alumni, he developed his talent until he had enriched the familiar essay with learning, wit, suavity, whimsy, and irony—all of a sort that demanded but well rewarded a relatively high level of reader understanding. Other writers were doing all this, but Benchley went farthest in building his pieces around a self-caricature of the author as a bumbler upset but unconquered by technology, mass media, and mass-man.

Benchley had his weaknesses and his obvious limitations. Despite his devotion to "freshness," there are stale sentences in his prose, usually because of a willingness to let three, five, or seven words participate where two, three, or four could have done the work. Like most humorists, he wrote too much on the same few themes and rewrote himself more and more frequently. More seriously, his range of subject matter and of feeling was narrow; he showed indignation at social abuses, but his work yields little pathos or suspense. Moreover, Benchley's bumbler is too incompetent and too well adjusted to his incompetence; his anxieties are petty even when stimulated by major problems. Fear, awe, crushing defeat, sex, joy, a sense of fate, or a vital awareness of the God in whom the author believed could not be conveyed through such a figure—at least were not so conveyed by Robert Benchley.

Some of these defects, however, have had a way of turning into virtues. Even without the pictorial drolleries of Gluyas Williams, the pompous figure of Benchley's Little Man would have worn deep grooves in the American consciousness—he is so utterly incompetent, and that incompetence is shown so completely and with such persistent, though sympathetic, irony in piece after piece. The effect of Benchley has inevitably merged with that of his contemporaries and followers, but it is no guess to say that the humorous monologue and the archetypal Little Man would have been very different, and poorer, without him.

Notes and References

Preface

1. Robert C. Benchley, "Books and Other Things," New York *World*, February 12, 1921, p. 10.
2. James Thurber, in "The Incomparable Mr. Benchley," *Credos and Curios*, Harper & Row (New York, and Evanston, Illinois, 1962), p. 147, has called Benchley "the humorist's humorist" and has quoted E. B. White's statement that White was sure he himself had imitated Benchley (148).

Chronology

1. Nathaniel Benchley, *Robert Benchley, a Biography*, McGraw-Hill (New York, 1955), p. 21. Andrew Forest Muir maintains that Robert's grandfather may actually have been pro-Confederate. See "The Skeleton in Bob Benchley's Closet," *Southwest Review*, XLIII (Winter, 1958), 70-72. Muir's case is more interesting than conclusive.
2. Gruening was cleared of all accusations by the Department of Justice and by Army Intelligence. (Nathaniel Benchley, *op. cit.* p. 127.)
3. Benchley was a dry in theory and practice—until Prohibition. See anon., "Benchley," *The New Yorker*, XXI (January 5, 1946), 18-19.
4. Nathaniel Benchley states that Robert appeared in forty-eight shorts and played in "and/or collaborated on" forty-seven feature pictures (181); but his list of shorts specified only forty-six titles (256-58).

Chapter One

1. Hamlin Hill, "Modern American Humor: the Janus Laugh," *College English*, XXV (December, 1963), 172-73.
2. Stephen Leacock, "Gertrude the Governess," in *Nonsense Novels* (New York and London, 1920), p. 77; see also *Laugh with Leacock* (New York), p. 131.
3. Oliver Wendell Holmes, *The Professor at the Breakfast-Table* (1860); *The Poet at the Breakfast-Table* (1872); *Over the Teacups* (1891).
4. Cited in Francis Hyde Bangs, *John Kendrick Bangs: Humorist of the Nineties* (New York, 1941), p. 131.

5. Holmes, *The Autocrat of the Breakfast-Table* (New York, 1961), p. 210.

6. *Ibid.*, pp. 267-76.

7. Edward W. Townsend, *"Chimmie Fadden," Major Max and Other Stories* (New York, 1895), pp. 31, 346. Bill Arp and Wallace Irwin (whose dialect *Letters of a Japanese Schoolboy,* 1907-1909, attracted much attention) were also among those who wrote humor both in dialect and in the language of "quality" magazine editorials.

8. *Puck,* XLVIII (August 15, 1900), 2. One of the crackerbox loafers asks if the other believes in home rule. The reply is, "Well, I dunno! Sometimes home rule jes' means lettin' the local machine do jes' as it durn pleases."

9. James Gray, "The Journalist as Literary Man," in May Brodbeck, James Gray, and Walter Metzger, *American Non-Fiction 1900-1950* (Chicago, 1952), p. 141.

10. *Love Conquers All,* p. 306. "The Conning Tower" was then appearing in the New York *World.* Thurber's contribution was published in December, 1926.

11. Francis Hyde Bangs, *John Kendrick Bangs,* pp. 36-55. Incidentally, *College Humor,* a magazine to which Benchley, Perelman, and other humorists occasionally contributed in the 1920's, featured, on the whole, humor of a sort that had little to do with college life.

12. The percentage of students of secondary-school age who were actually attending such schools rose from about ten in 1905 to sixty in 1935. See James Mulhern, *A History of Education* (New York, 1946), p. 611. This rise in the educational level of the potential readership for humor probably had more to do with changes in reading tastes and hence in writing style and content than the even more rapid rise in college and university attendance. However, one staff writer for *Life,* at the time it was founded in 1883, felt that the campuses were indeed furnishing a high-level readership of their own: "There was no periodical appealing to that spirit of gaiety, satire, and humor which the Harvard *Lampoon* had been the first to cultivate." See Robert Bridges, "The First Years," *Life,* LXXXI (January 4, 1923), 23.

13. Frederick Lewis Allen, "Cart Before the Horse," *Century,* XC (October, 1915), 942-51. Allen wrote most of his humorous stories and essays before acquiring distinction as a historian and as editor of *Harper's Magazine.*

14. Robert Benchley, "The Theatre," *The New Yorker,* XII (October 24, 1936), 26.

15. Harvard *Lampoon,* LXII (November 24, 1911), 165.

16. Nathaniel Benchley, *op. cit.,* p. 43. At Harvard, Robert definitely considered himself an artist rather than a writer. The figures

on his drawing and writing do not include Vol. LXIII. Many of the contributions to the *Lampoon* were not by-lined and are identifiable only because the author's or artist's name is given in the index. Vol. LXIII has no index.

17. *Ibid.* p. 39. Nathaniel adds, "It didn't matter that all of the character looked Irish, because at that time a joke wasn't considered funny unless it was about an Irishman, Negro, or a German." See also *Lampoon*, LXI (June 9, 1911), 238, and LVIII (February 4, 1910), 272, 273. Nevertheless, as noted earlier, dialect humor appeared sparingly in the essays, narratives, and verse.

18. Cited in Walter Blair, *Native American Humor* (San Francisco, 1960), p. 427.

19. *Lampoon*, LXI (May 6, 1911), 154.

20. *Lampoon*, LVIII (December 21, 1909), 182; LX (October 28, 1910), 77; LXII (February 6, 1912), 344-45; LXII (December 11, 1911), 224-25; LXI (March 3, 1911), 16-17, 19.

21. Walter Blair, *Native American Humor,* p. 171, and *Horse Sense in American Humor* (Chicago, 1943), pp. 274-77; see also John C. Gerber, "Mark Twain's Use of the Comic Pose," *PMLA,* LXXVII (June, 1962), 297-304.

22. For examples of papers on "the Idiot," see John Kendrick Bangs, *Coffee and Repartee and the Idiot,* (New York and London, 1900). *Coffee and Repartee* was first published in 1893. See also Ralph L. Curry, "Leacock and Benchley: an Acknowledged Literary Debt," *American Book Collector,* VII (March, 1957), 14, and *Stephen Leacock* (Garden City, New York, 1959), p. 83; and Leacock, "My Financial Career," *Laugh with Leacock,* 1-4; also the tribute from Benchley as cited, p. vi.

23. See Irvin S. Cobb, *Cobb's Anatomy* (New York, 1912); *Cobb's Bill of Fare* (New York, 1913), and *"Speaking of Operations—"* (New York, 1915).

24. See A. A. Milne, *Not That It Matters,* 10th edition (London, 1933; the 1st edition appeared in 1919), especially pp. 1, 75-79. Benchley praises Milne's nondramatic humor in "Books and Other Things," New York *World* (December 6, 1920), p. 12.

25. Nathaniel Benchley, *op. cit.,* pp. 217, 22.

26. *Ibid.,* pp. 39-41.

27. Robert Benchley, "Ivy Oration," reprinted in *The Harvard "Advocate" Anthology,* ed. Donald Hall, (New York, 1950), pp. 128-34. Nathaniel Benchley, in *Robert Benchley* (p. 48), says that Robert discarded most of the prepared text and ad-libbed his way through the speech. The present comments are, of course, based on the printed version, which represents what Benchley could do on paper at this time. In a note to the present writer, Nathaniel adds

that at the opening of the speech, Robert shouted "Surprise!" and then waited a while before going on.

28. Finley Peter Dunne, *Mr. Dooley in Peace and in War* (Boston, 1898), pp. 25, 48.

29. Grammarians like to subdivide faulty parallelisms in English under labels derived from ancient Greek, such as *syllepsis, zeugma,* and *chiasmus.* One would like to know how Benchley would have subdivided grammarians.

30. Frederick L. Allen, "The Goon and His Style," *Harper's Magazine,* CXLIV (December, 1921), 121-22.

31. Nathaniel Benchley, *op. cit.,* p. 97.

32. William Lee Miller, "There Really Was a Benchley," *Reporter,* XIV (January 12, 1956), 39.

33. Robert Benchley, "What College Did to Me," *The Early Worm* (New York, 1927), pp. 69-77.

34. *Pluck and Luck,* 174-85, 26-35; *The Benchley Roundup,* 124-29. See also Robert Benchley, "The Theatre," *The New Yorker,* XII (December 26, 1936), 26, 28, as well as his caustic remarks on other plays about college life, in "The Theatre," *The New Yorker,* XIV (November 26, 1938), 28.

35. Clarence B. Randall, economist, cited by John G. Fuller, "Trade Winds," *Saturday Review,* XLVI (April 20, 1963), 8, 10.

Chapter Two

1. Nathaniel Benchley, *op. cit.,* p. 81.

2. *Ibid.,* pp. 81-82.

3. *Ibid.,* p. 55.

4. "Publicity Playlets. No. I: A Comedy in Two Acts," *Obiter Dicta,* I (May, 1913), 25. Through the cooperation of Mr. Frank Strohkarck, of the Curtis Publishing Company, I have been able to get photocopies of the magazine. The original file is in the possession of the firm.

5. *Obiter Dicta,* I (June, 1913), 37-38; I (July-August, 1913), 42-43.

6. *The Ring Lardner Reader,* ed. Maxwell˙ Geismar (New York, 1963), p. 602.

7. S. J. Perelman, *The Most of S. J. Perelman,* (New York, 1958), p. 245.

8. The nonsense in *Obiter Dicta* usually has satirical elements and thus is not pure nonsense. The relation of nonsense to satire is discussed in Chapter 8.

9. James Thurber, *The Years with Ross* (Boston, Toronto, 1959), p. 188.

10. Nathaniel Benchley, *op. cit.,* p. 62.

11. *20,000 Leagues Under the Sea* (New York, 1928), pp. 212-19.
12. Nathaniel Benchley, *op. cit.*, pp. 83, 94-100.
13. Nathaniel Benchley, *op. cit.*, pp. 23-24.
14. *Ibid.*, pp. 125-27; Senator Ernest Gruening to Norris W. Yates, April 15, 1964.
15. John Macy, untitled review, *Bookman*, XXIX (May, 1909), 311-12.
16. See Chapter 10, Note 14.
17. Thurber says of Benchley that "... there was nobody whose praise a cartoonist or humorist would rather have had." See James Thurber, *The Years With Ross*, p. 55.
18. In "The Incomparable Mr. Benchley," *Credos and Curios* (New York and Evanston, 1962), pp. 146-52, Thurber quotes praise of Robert as a forerunner and example by E. B. White, Frank Sullivan, Wolcott Gibbs, and other mainstays of *The New Yorker*.
19. R. C. Benchley, "Football Phenomena," *Collier's*, LVI (November 20, 1915), 32. Cf. his "Vox Populi" (December 25, 1915), 21 (reprinted in *Chips Off the Old Benchley*), pp. 234-35, and "Of Indoor Sports," LVI (January 8, 1916), 81.
20. Nathaniel Benchley, *op. cit.*, p. 79.
21. Paul R. Reynolds to Robert C. Benchley, October 9, 1915, and November 10, 1915; in the possession of Mrs. Gertrude D. Benchley.

Chapter Three

1. Nathaniel Benchley, *op. cit.*, p. 100.
2. "The Theatre," *Life*, XCIII (March 29, 1929), 20.
3. Nathaniel Benchley, *op. cit.*, p. 101.
4. Mark Sullivan, *Our Times: the United States 1900-1925*, Vol. I, (New York and London, 1928), p. 1. See also "Have You a Little German Agent in Your Home?" *Vanity Fair*, X (March, 1918), 51, 106. This piece was one of several published by Benchley under the pseudonym of "Brighton Perry."
5. "Football Phenomena," *Collier's*, LVI (November 20, 1915), 32; reprinted in *Chips Off the Old Benchley*, pp. 222-31.
6. "America's Greatest Movement: the Jaw Movement," *World Outlook*, II (October, 1916), 8-9.
7. "Vox Populi," *Collier's*, LVI (December 25, 1915), 21; see also LVI, "Of Indoor Sports" (January 8, 1916), 81.
8. "The Making of a Red," *Nation*, CVIII (March 15, 1919), 399-400. Cf. James Thurber, "The Very Proper Gander," *The Thurber Carnival* (New York and London, 1945), p. 251. For two more of Benchley's blasts, see *20,000 Leagues Under the Sea*, pp. 138-41, and *Of All Things!* (New York, 1921), pp. 182-84.

9. Edgar Kemler, *The Irreverent Mr. Mencken* (Boston, 1950), pp. 191-216; Francis Russell, *Tragedy in Dedham, the Story of the Sacco-Vanzetti Case* (New York, 1962), pp. 391, 412.

10. Reprinted in *Chips Off the Old Benchley*, pp. 301-06, with 1917 cited as date of copyright. In Washington, Benchley partially overcame his distrust of nature and worked with Ernest Gruening in successfully raising "lettuce, chard, radishes, early peas, and parsley." See Nathaniel Benchley, *op. cit.*, p. 121.

11. "The Will to Suffer," *Bellman*, XXII (March 17, 1917), 297-98.

12. Charles A. Fenton, "A Literary Fracture of World War I," *American Quarterly*, XII (Summer, 1960), 119-32.

13. *Ibid.*, p. 139.

14. Randolph Bourne, "Twilight of the Idols," *Seven Arts* (October, 1917), reprinted in *Untimely Papers*, B. W. Huebsch (New York, 1919), 114-39.

15. *Treat 'Em Rough: Letters from Jack the Kaiser Killer*, Bobbs-Merrill (Indianapolis, 1918), and *The Real Dope*, Bobbs-Merrill (Indianapolis, 1919).

16. Don Marquis, *Poems and Portraits*, (Garden City, New York, 1922), p. 90-93, 96-97.

17. Nathaniel Benchley, *op. cit.*, p. 133.

18. Pre-war humorists whose careers were little impaired by the conflict included Clarence Day, Jr., Irvin S. Cobb, Octavus Roy Cohen, Montague Glass, and Harry Leon Wilson.

Chapter Four

1. *The Portable Ring Lardner*, p. 735.

2. John Jay Chapman, "A New Menace to Education," *Vanity Fair*, XII (June, 1919), 27, 88.

3. Nathaniel Benchley, *op. cit.*, p. 136. "Crownie's" objections to the innocuous passage on the mating of newts is odd in view of his liberality toward nude art in *Vanity Fair*. The cover drawing of the February, 1929, number is a nude worthy of *Playboy*.

4. "Mr. Vanity Fair," *Bookman*, L (January, 1920), 429-33. Benchley was not afraid to imply criticism of Crowninshield in this article, but he closed with, "It is much simpler to describe a magazine than a man, especially when the man happens to be your boss."

5. *The Thurber Carnival*, p. 175.

6. "Have You Tried These New Memory Courses?" *Vanity Fair*, XII (June, 1919), 50. Cf. *The Thurber Carnival*, pp. 49-50, where Mitty tries to use word association as an aid to memory: " 'Toothpaste, toothbrush, bicarbonate, carborundum, initiative and referen-

dum?'" Not until he calls the district attorney in one of his day-dreams a "'miserable cur'" does he remember what his wife wanted him to buy "'puppy biscuit.'"

7. Nathaniel Benchley, *op. cit.*, p. 137.

8. Dorothy Parker's relatively mild strictures on Miss Burke—mild considering Dorothy's gifts of wit and invective—are in *Vanity Fair*, XIII (January, 1929), 94, and are cited by Nathaniel Benchley, p. 143.

9. Nathaniel Benchley, *op. cit.*, p. 145.

10. New York *World* (February 9, 1920), p. 8.

11. *Ibid.* (November 22, 1920), p. 10; (April 12, 1920), p. 8. Both pieces reappeared in *Love Conquers All*, pp. 274-76, 303-06.

12. *World* (November 8, 1920), p. 10; (November 18, 1920), p.16; (November 24, 1920), p. 12.

13. *Ibid.* (December 4, 1920), p. 10; cf. Robert C. Benchley, "Heroes of Realism," *The Bookman*, LII (February, 1921), 559-60.

14. *World* (July 10, 1920), p. 8.

15. *Ibid.* (November 24, 1920), p. 10.

16. *Ibid.* (December 18, 1920), p. 12.

17. See "Drama," *Life*, LXXXV (March 12, 1925), 20, where, in reviewing the production of Joyce's play *Exiles*, Benchley said, "We now understand why Mr. Joyce wrote 'Ulysses' in the incoherent style that he did. When he puts his words together so that they make sense, as he has done in *Exiles*, they sound just like ordinary writing. Very ordinary writing."

18. Gertrude D. Benchley (Mrs. Robert Benchley) to Norris W. Yates, May 18, 1964. The syndicate was the Consolidated Press Association, headed by David Lawrence; and there is no record that Benchley worked for Lawrence beyond the six months stipulated in the contract.

19. Nathaniel Benchley, *op. cit.*, p. 150.

20. *Credos and Curios*, p. 148.

21. In 1929, when Benchley left, the circulation was about 116,000—not bad, really, for a quality weekly in the year of the crash. *Life* was still in the black when Henry Luce bought the title in 1936. Luce terminated the magazine and began his own quite different periodical.

22. Benchley as a critic of the theater is discussed by Nathaniel Benchley, pp. 150-53, 169-74; and in Norris W. Yates, *The American Humorist: Conscience of the Twentieth Century* (Ames, Iowa, 1964), pp. 248-52; the latter also includes comments on Robert's criticism of non-dramatic literature.

23. "Drama," *Life*, LXXVIII (June 16, 1921), 876 (about O'Neill's *Gold*).

24. "The Theatre," *The New Yorker*, VI (March 8, 1930), 27-28.

25. Reprinted in Bernard Hewitt, *Theatre U. S. A.*, (New York, 1959), p. 341.

26. "The Theatre," *The New Yorker*, VII (November 7, 1931), 28. A warm supporter of O'Neill's reputation from *Beyond the Horizon* through *Mourning Becomes Electra*, Benchley had reservations about *The Hairy Ape*, *Dynamo*, and *Strange Interlude*. His review of *Dynamo* is reprinted in *O'Neill and His Plays*, ed. Oscar Cargill, N. Bryllion Fagin, and William J. Fisher, New York Univerity (New York, 1961), pp. 187-89.

27. "Drama," *Life*, LXXVII (January 27, 1921), 136.

28. *Ibid.*, LXXVII (June 2, 1921), 800-01.

29. Nathaniel Benchley, *op. cit.*, p. 170; "Drama," *Life*, LXXVIII (December 22, 1921), 18.

30. Nathaniel Benchley, *op. cit.*, p. 170. Using terms coined by George Jean Nathan and Sinclair Lewis, Benchley struck at "bronchial boobery" as practiced in the theater by citizens of "Cougher Prairie." See *Life*, LXXVIII (December 22, 1921), 18.

31. "The Theatre," *The New Yorker*, VI (November 29, 1930), 36.

32. *Ibid.*, VI (May 10, 1930), 32.

33. "Drama," *Life*, LXXIX (March 10, 1927), 21.

34. *Ibid.*, LXXVII (June 23, 1921), 912.

35. Nathaniel Benchley, *op. cit.*, p. 190-91; also personal interview with Nathaniel Benchley, February 28, 1963.

Chapter Five

1. New York *World* (December 6, 1920), p. 12.

2. On Lardner, see Benchley's "The Fate of the Funny Men," *Bookman*, LVIII (June, 1923), 455-57. For Benchley on Perelman, see Blair, *Horse Sense in American Humor*, p. 283, and *Native American Humor,* p. 176.

3. *Ibid.*, p..171; cf. *Horse Sense in American Humor*, pp. 274-83, also Bernard DeVoto, "The Lineage of Eustace Tilley," *Saturday Review of Literature*, XVI (September 25, 1937), 20.

4. *My Ten Years in a Quandary* (New York, 1936), p. 26.

5. J. Bryan III, "Funny Man: a Study in Professional Frustration," *Saturday Evening Post*, CCXII (September 23, 1939), 11; Sigmund Freud, *Civilization and Its Discontents* (Garden City, New York, n. d.), p. 27; Karen Horney, *The Neurotic Personality of Our Time* (New York, 1937), p. 99.

6. "On Being an American," in *H. L. Mencken Prejudices: a Selection*, ed. James T. Farrell (New York, 1958), p. 90; *Life*, LXXVII (September 8, 1921), 3. Benchey almost certainly wrote the prospectus for this issue of the magazine.

7. Quoted by Richard Hofstadter, *Anti-Intellectualism in American Life* (New York, 1964), p. 367. The cult of the child is discussed in detail, pp. 359-90.

8. *World* (May 18, 1920), p. 14; *Pluck and Luck;* 197-203. cf. Frances Hodgson Burnett, *Editha's Burglar: a Story for Children* (Boston, 1888).

9. Harvard *Lampoon,* LXII (November 24, 1911), 151.

10. Nathaniel Benchley, *op. cit.,* pp. 192-93. A minor example of how Benchley's humor gained in astringency after his university efforts may be seen in how Tiny Tim's "God bless us, every one"—cited in another *Lampoon* editorial, LXI, (June 22, 1911), 271—became, in the much later "Christmas Afternoon," "God help us, every one."

11. Henry F. May, *The End of American Innocence* 1912-1917 (New York, 1961), especially Chaper I; *Collected Edition of Heywood Broun,* comp. Heywood Hale Broun, (New York, 1941), pp. 52-61; James Thurber, "News of the Day, And a Little Child—", *The New Yorker,* III (April 2, 1927), 34. See also Thurber's version of Little Red Riding Hood, "The Little Girl and the Wolf," from *Fables for Our Time,* reprinted in *The Thurber Carnival,* p. 247.

12. Yates, *The American Humorist,* pp. 38-43, 246-47, 253. For Benchley's war against nature, see also Frank Sullivan, "Introduction" to *Chips Off the Old Benchley,* xviii-xix.

13. Frank Sullivan, "Introduction" to *Chips Off the Old Benchley,* p. xviii.

14. *Of All Things!,* p. 44; Nathaniel Benchley, *op. cit.,* pp. 200-01.

15. *The Early Worm* (New York, 1927), p. 5.

16. Edward Godfrey, "A Hike and a Boatride," *Stories and Poems Read by Uncle Ed Over KDKA* (Pittsburgh, 1926), pp. 52-53. The date of this broadcast was October 26, 1923.

17. *Of All Things!,* 103-04.

18. Anon., "Benchley," *The New Yorker,* XXI (January 5, 1946), 18.

19. Nathaniel Benchley, *op. cit.,* 181-82. When the banks were having troubles, he wrote, "I can see no possible grounds in the future on which the practical man of affairs can criticize a playwright or an author for being 'flighty' or 'crack-brained.' It has been a great year for the reestablishment of *amour propre* among dreamers with inferiorities." See "The Theatre," *The New Yorker,* IX (March 11, 1933), 26, 28.

20. *The Treasurer's Report,* pp. 191-201. "From Nine to Five" originally appeared in *Collier's,* LXIII (May 3, 1919), 9, 38-39, three years before *Babbitt* was published. It is reprinted in *The Benchley Roundup,* pp. 26-32. See also "How to Understand International Finance," *Love Conquers All,* pp. 157-59.

21. *Nathaniel Benchley, op. cit.,* pp. 16, 63-64, 163-64.

22. *Ibid.,* p. 194.

23. Frederick Lewis Allen, *The Big Change* (New York, 1961), pp. 116-28 (original ed., New York, 1952). See also Allen's *Only Yesterday* (New York, 1952), especially pp. 138-41.

24. *Life,* LXXVIII (October 13, 1921), 3.

25. Donald Day, *Will Rogers: a Biography* (New York, 1962), pp. 231-36; Will Rogers, *Life,* XCI (May 31, 1928), 3 and XCI (June 21, 1928), 3-4. For humorous contributions to the Anti-Bunk campaign by Benchley, see *20,000 Leagues Under the Sea,* pp. 3-6, 66-69, 138-41, 178-81, 190-92.

26. Such topical pieces as "Spy Scares," *My Ten Years in a Quandary,* pp. 207-10, are infrequent.

27. Guy Fawkes [pseudonym of Benchley], "The Wayward Press," *The New Yorker,* XIII (March 13, 1937), 40, 42; XII (November 14, 1936), 88. The idea of "The Wayward Press" department bears symptoms of having developed gradually. A piece by Benchley, "The Unsung Heroes," in *The New Yorker,* III (June 19, 1927), 38, dealt with the problems of reporters who had to write virtually the same story over and over concerning the receptions of Lindbergh and of Clarence Chamberlain in one European country after another. A separate piece on the same page, by "R. B.," commented on the look of Coolidge's "yachting cap" when the President was inspecting the fleet—a minor matter but likewise having to do with propaganda and the press. An article by "Horace Greeley, Jr.," entitled "The Press in Review," *The New Yorker,* III (July 2, 1927), 28, 30, acidulously summarizes the orgy of flapdoodle in the press over Lindbergh. The first use of "Guy Fawkes" as a pseudonym, presumably by Benchley, likewise bears the title, "The Press in Review," III (July 23, 1927), 28, 30, 32; it opens with praise for the sober handling in the New York newspapers of Byrd's flight in the *America.* The same issue also has "Force of Habit" (p. 19), a parody by Benchley, over his own name, of how Grover Whalen in New York and the Lord Mayor in London received transatlantic fliers. Thereafter, four more commentaries by "Guy Fawkes," all entitled "The Press in Review," occur (August 13, September 3, October 8, November 5) before the first use of the head "The Wayward Press." The first article under this head appeared in III (December 24, 1927), 23-24, over the name of Guy Fawkes. Apparently the scheme for a column evaluating various news stories developed out of the comments by Benchley and possibly others on the press coverage of the transatlantic flights and of their consequences.

28. "The Theatre," *The New Yorker,* XV (January 20, 1940), 20, 32.

29. "Books and Other Things," New York *World* (February 14, 1920), 8. See also the *World* (December 15, 1920), 14.

30. *Ibid.*, (December 22, 1920), 12.

31. *The Thurber Carnival*, pp. 174-75. Thurber's comment represented his attitude more accurately in 1933, when it was written, than in the later thirties, when more concern for national and world trends was reflected in his writing.

32. *Chips Off the Old Benchley*, p. 193.

33. *World* (April 14, 1920), p. 12, reprinted in *Love Conquers All*, pp. 206-10. *World* (August 24, 1920), p. 8. Nathaniel Benchley says of his father, "He spent several lunch hours in Harlem, investigating housing conditions for the Urban League, but he wasn't particularly effective because he didn't want to interview the tenants in too much detail. He said about one building on East 112th Street that 'they were all such clean and respectable people that I felt that I had no call to put them through the third degree'" (pp. 63-64). The passage reveals something of the sensitivity of the man behind the bumbling persona. For discussion of the National Urban League (an ancestor of the NAACP), see Gilbert Osofsky, "Progressivism and the Negro: New York, 1900-1915," *American Quarterly*, XVI (Summer, 1964), 153-68.

34. Ironically, the very next year Mrs. Vorse published *Men and Steel*, a novel based on the Lawrence, Massachusetts, textile strike of 1912; and her writing since that book has been marked by a strong social conscience, e.g., *Strike: a Novel of Gastonia* (New York, 1930).

35. "The Theatre," *The New Yorker*, IX (March 11, 1933), 26, 28.

36. *Ibid.*, IX (April 15, 1933), 24.

37. *"Drama,"* Life, LXXVII (January 13, 1921), 64.

38. *Ibid.*, LXXXIII (March 27, 1924), 18.

39. *Ibid.*, LXXIX (May 25, 1922), 18.

40. "The Emancipation Proclamation," *Life*, LXXVI (September 9, 1920), 449.

41. *Credos and Curios*, pp. 148-49.

42. *20,000 Leagues Under the Sea*, p. 3.

43. *The Early Worm*, p. 103.

44. For Marquis, statistics classified themselves in colors: sevens suggested red, and fives were yellow. See Don Marquis, "Preface to a Book of Statistics," *Prefaces* (New York, 1923), pp. 183-89.

45. James Thurber, *Let Your Mind Alone!* (New York and London, 1937), p. 161. For a classic statement, by a leading novelist, of the need to reconcile the scientific approach with man's actual life experiences, see John Steinbeck and Edward F. Ricketts, *Sea of Cortez* (New York, 1941), pp. 2-3.

46. "All About Relativity," *Vanity Fair*, XIV (March, 1920), 61. The shift of light toward the red end of the spectrum is described ironically as "self-evident." Cf. *World* (October 16, 1920), p. 12; "How Much Does the Sun Jump?" *Pluck and Luck*, 251-54, and "Is There Really a Moon?" *After 1903—What?*, 246-47.

47. Cf. "Do Insects Think?"; *Love Conquers All*, 62-64; "Justice for Mussels!" *Pluck and Luck*, 265-67, and "Evolution Sidelights," *ibid.*, 274-77. See also Nathaniel Benchley *op. cit.*, 137.

48. See note 27, this chapter.

49. *The Benchley Roundup*, p. 217.

50. For example, see John Q. Anderson, ed., *Louisiana Swamp Doctor* (Baton Rouge, Louisiana, 1962), and Arthur Palmer Hudson, ed. *Humor of the Old Deep South* (New York, 1936), pp. 126-50.

51. Allen, *The Big Change*, p. 177.

52. Finley Peter Dunne, *Mr. Dooley's Opinions* (New York, 1901), pp. 3-9; Stephen Leacock, *Literary Lapses* (London, 1910), pp. 54-61; Irvin S. Cobb, "*Speaking of Operations—*" (Garden City, New York, 1915); Will Rogers, *Ether and Me* (New York, 1929).

53. Nathaniel Benchley, *op. cit.*, pp. 13-14.

54. From *Bed to Worse*, pp. 197-200; "The Theatre," *The New Yorker*, X (March 17, 1934), 32, 34; "Swat the Tsk-Tsk Midge!" *No Poems*, pp. 22-28; "Stamp Out Schistosomiasis!" *After 1903—What?*, pp. 136-39.

55. "Books and Other Things," New York *World* (September 22, 1920), 12.

56. *My Ten Years in a Quandary*, p. 34. Cf. "How Insane Are You?" *Of All Things!*, pp. 218-19; "Measure Your Mind," *Love Conquers All*, pp. 298-302; "My Subconscious," *Chips Off the Old Benchley*, pp. 292-94; "Do Dreams Go by Opposites?" *My Ten Years in a Quandary*, pp. 49-52.

57. *World* (January 22, 1921), 10.

58. Nathaniel Benchley, *op. cit.*, p. 190.

59. *Ibid.*, p. 186.

60. Lowell Thomas doubted Rogers' "pretense that he was an ignorant and illiterate fellow," and correctly pointed out that "Rogers' writings from time to time betrayed an exceedingly wide knowledge." See P. J. O'Brien, *Will Rogers* (Chicago, 1935), p. 8.

61. *20,000 Leagues Under the Sea*, p.88.

62. *The Benchley Roundup*, pp. 51-56, 108-10.

63. *Chips Off the Old Benchley*, p. 134.

64. *The Early Worm*, p. 17.

65. *My Ten Years in a Quandary*, p. 166.

66. See Howard Webb, "The Meaning of Ring Lardner's Fiction: a Re-Evaluation," *American Literature*, XXXI (January, 1960), 434-45,

also Peter DeVries, "James Thurber: the Comic Prufrock," *Poetry* LXIII (December, 1943), 150-59.

Chapter Six

1. E. B. White, *The Second Tree from the Corner,* Harper (New York, 1954), p. 173, revised from E. B. White and Katharine S. White, *A Subtreasury of American Humor,* Random House (New York, 1948), p. xvii. The bibliographies in Gilbert Highet, *The Anatomy of Satire* (Princeton, New Jersey, 1962), and Leonard Feinberg, *The Satirist* (Ames, Iowa, 1963), and *An Introduction to Satire* (Ames Iowa, 1967), especially the two books by Feinberg, give the venturesome a good start into the jungle of speculation about the nature of humor and satire.

2. *World* (February 12, 1921), 10.

3. "Why We Laugh—or Do We?" *After 1903—What?,* p. 47. Though the proposition that individuals differ widely and mysteriously in their responses to humor seems self-evident, for a contrary view see Max Eastman, *Enjoyment of Laughter* (London, 1939), p. 378. See also Northrope Frye, *The Anatomy of Criticism* (Princeton, 1957): "Humor, like attack, is founded on convention" (p. 225). Moreover, according to Evelyn Waugh and W. H. Auden, the conventions must be shared by reader and writer. See Feinberg, *The Satirist,* pp. 303-04.

4. Stephen Leacock, *Humor: Its Theory and Technique,* Dodd, Mead (New York, 1935), pp. 1-15; idem, *Humor and Humanity,* Henry Holt (New York, 1938), "Preface" (no pagination), and p. 108. For Eastman's criticisms of Benchley, see *Enjoyment of Laughter,* pp. 335-36.

5. Nathaniel Benchley, *op. cit.,* pp. 115-16, 168-69.

6. *Ibid.,* p. 17.

7. "Mr. Vanity Fair," *Bookman,* L (January, 1920), 429-33.

8. "The Brow-Elevation in Humor," *Love Conquers All,* 300-06.

9. Leo Marx, "The Vernacular Tradition in American Literature," *Studies in American Culture,* ed. Joseph J. Kwiatt and Mary C. Turpie, University of Minnesota (Minneapolis, 1960), pp. 109-22.

10. "Pretty Dull Reading," *Life,* LXXXVIII (June 19, 1926), 19.

11. *Loc. cit.*

12. *Of All Things!,* p. 198; *The Early Worm,* pp. 214, 157.

13. "Comedy After Midnight," *Life,* LXXXVIII (July 29, 1926), 19.

14. *Loc. cit.,* see also "The Theatre," *The New Yorker,* VI (October 4, 1930), 34, 36, 38, and further praise of Durante by Benchley in "The Theatre," *The New Yorker,* VI (December 20, 1930), 30.

15. Edmund Wilson, *A Literary Chronicle, 1920-1950* (Garden City, New York, 1956), p. 54.

16. *The Benchley Roundup*, p. 109.

17. "Home Made Jokes," *After 1903—What?*, pp. 98-99. In his monologues for the movies Benchley's customary mask of smug seriousness was occasionally—but only occasionally—broken by grimaces of shock, distaste, or pained resignation.

18. Nathaniel Benchley, *op. cit.*, p. 190.

19. *Life*, LXXXI (January 4, 1923), 26-27; reprinted in *Pluck and Luck*, pp. 157-60.

20. *After 1903—What?*, pp. 48-49.

21. *Pluck and Luck*, p. 157.

22. *World* (April 5, 1920), p. 12; see Max Beerbohm, *Seven Men* (London, 1919), pp. 3-48.

23. "The Personal Service of Mr. Ed Wynn," *Life*, LXXV (May 6, 1920), 842-43; "Drama," *Life*, LXXVIII (July 14, 1921), 18.

24. "Drama," *Life*, LXXV (May 13, 1920), 896-97; LXXVI (October 14, 1920), 680.

25. Marginal notation by Nathaniel Benchley on carbon copy of final typescript of this book, p. 157. In the possession of Norris W. Yates. For further praise of Chaplin by Robert Benchley, see "Drama," *Life*, LXXV (May 13, 1920), 896-97, but for implied criticism through parody, see Robert C. Benchley, "Hamlet for Broadway," *Vanity Fair*, V (January, 1916), 67.

26. "Drama," *Life*, LXXXIII (July 3, 1924), 18.

27. "Drama," *Life*, LXXIX (June 29, 1922), 18.

28. Eastman, *Enjoyment of Laughter*, pp. 249-57; Highet, *The Anatomy of Satire*, pp. 42-43 and *passim*.

29. Nathaniel Benchley, *op. cit.*, p. 77.

30. "The Theatre," *The New Yorker*, XIV (January 14, 1939), 28, 30.

31. "The Theatre," *The New Yorker*, VI (November 29, 1930), 36.

32. *The Anatomy of Satire*, pp. 18, 103, and *passim*.

33. In the spring of 1964, Richard Schickel received a Guggenheim grant to do a much-needed study of the comic novel in America. His findings about the comic romances of Harry Leon Wilson, Booth Tarkington, and Clarence Budington Kelland, the naughtier novels of Cabell, Erskine, *et al*, and the "dark comedians" or "black humorists" Joseph Heller, Bruce Jay Friedman, John Barth, Richard Stern, Thomas Pynchon, and J. P. Dunleavy will be awaited with interest.

34. "I share Ross's deep conviction that major blasphemies have no place in comedy" (Thurber, *The Years with Ross*, p. 50). The censors never scissored Will Rogers' movies because Will saw to it that they never needed sanitizing, and he withdrew from the stage

cast of *Ah, Wilderness!* because of a single letter objecting to one scene. Lardner conducted a one-man crusade in *The New Yorker* for cleaner lyrics in popular songs sung over the radio. See Donald Day, *Will Rogers*, pp. 333, 338-39; Donald Elder, *Ring Lardner*, pp. 349-59.

35. "Je me presse de rire de tout, de peur d'etre obligé d'en pleurer." From *Le Barbier de Séville*, I, ii, in *Theatre de Beaumarchais*, Garnier Fréres (Librairies Editeurs, Paris, n. d.), p. 33.

36. James Thurber, *The Thurber Carnival* (New York and London, 1945), p. 174.

37. Groucho Marx, *Groucho and Me* (Third Printing, New York, 1959), pp. 88-89. This tale has also been told concerning Grimaldi and other famous clowns.

38. Benchley, "The Silent Art of Joe Jackson," *Everybody's Magazine*, XLIV (February, 1921), 31; "Drama," *Life*, LXXV (May 13, 1920), 896-97.

39. Dunne, *Mr. Dooley in Peace and in War*, p. 151.

40. Ring Lardner, "There Are Smiles," *Round Up* (New York, 1929), pp. 271-281.

41. *The Anatomy of Satire*, p. 231.

Chapter Seven

1. *The Benchley Roundup*, p. 140.
2. *My Ten Years in a Quandary*, p. 170.
3. *Ibid.*, p. 283.
4. E. B. White, *One Man's Meat*, (New York, 1950), p. 163. White's comment was first published in June, 1940.
5. *Mr. Dooley in Peace and in War*, pp. 236, 237.
6. *My Ten Years in a Quandary*, p. 282.
7. *Ibid.*, p. 283.
8. *Pluck and Luck*, p. 100.
9. Gilbert Highet, *The Anatomy of Satire* (Princeton, 1962), pp. 13-14, 52-61, especially p. 53.
10. Constance Rourke, *American Humor* (New York, 1931), pp. 229-30.
11. "The Lottery Man," *Harvard Advocate* (March, 1911), reprinted in *The Harvard "Advocate" Anthology*, pp. 127-28; "Minutes in the Courses," *Lampoon*, LXI (May 24, 1911), 188; "Ivy Oration," *The Harvard "Advocate" Anthology*, pp. 128-34; see also Nathaniel Benchley, *op. cit.*, pp. 2-41.
12. *My Ten Years in a Quandary*, p. 321.
13. As a supply officer in the Navy during World War I, MacGregor *did* "lose" a locomotive (Personal interview with Nathaniel Benchley, February 28, 1963).

14. *The Most of S. J. Perelman* (New York, 1957), pp. 185-90.
15. Nathaniel Benchley, *op. cit.*, pp. 98-99.
16. "Mr. Vanity Fair," *Bookman*, L (January, 1920), 429-33.
17. Clarence Day, Jr., *The Crow's Nest* (New York, 1921), pp. 77-83, 84-88, 142-46. In these examples, the openings consume one-third to one-half of the essays.
18. Alexander Woollcott, *Going to Pieces* (New York and London, 1928), pp. 152-66, 240-46.

Chapter Eight

1. *Credos and Curios*, p. 150.
2. Personal interview with Nathaniel Benchley, February 28, 1963.
3. *After 1903—What?*, p. 194. Cf. "Horse-Sense Editorial," *Pluck and Luck*, pp. 54-61, and "Maxims from the Chinese," *My Ten Years in a Quandary*, pp. 215-17. See also "The Passing of the Orthodox Paradox," *Of All Things!* pp. 168-74—a parody of the Oscar Wilde-Noel Coward way of tossing epigrams to and fro in drawing-room comedies.
4. *Life*, LXXXI (January 11, 1923), 19; LXXXI (March 18, 1923), 19. The comment on *Scandal* is a take-off on the titles of "pure books on avoided subjects" by Sylvanus Stall—e. g., *What a Young Girl Ought to Know*.
5. *Of All Things!*, p. 184. Cf. *After 1903—What?*, p. 148, and *Pluck and Luck*, p. 76—"The elevated train in the background at the right was the first run under its own conflagration."
6. *My Ten Years in a Quandary*, p. 279.
7. *Inside Benchley*, p. 13.
8. *My Ten Years in a Quandary*, p. 169.
9. *Ibid.*, p. 218.
10. *After 1903—What?*, p. 45.
11. *The Thurber Carnival*, p. 48. Cf. The spoonerism "shaw the sipment" committed by the "efficient" businessman, in *Of All Things!*, p. 93.
12. *The Early Worm*, p. 4.
13. *The Treasurer's Report*, pp. 338-39.
14. *The Benchley Roundup*, p. 214.
15. *Of All Things!* p. 157.
16. *The Treasurer's Report*, p. 253.
17. *After 1903—What?*, pp. 42-47.
18. *The Benchley Roundup*, pp. 26-32.
19. *Ibid.*, p. 61.
20. *After 1903—What?*, p. 208.
21. *The Benchley Roundup*, p. 60.

22. *The Lovingood Papers*, II, ed. Ben Harris McClary (Knoxville, 1963), p. 46; see also pp. 23, 30, 60.

23. Mody C. Boatright, *Folk Laughter on the American Frontier* (New York, 1929), p. 91.

24. *20,000 Leagues Under the Sea*, p. 181.

25. *Pluck and Luck*, p. 23.

26. *My Ten Years in a Quandary*, p. 150.

27. *After 1903—What?* pp. 90-91.

28. *Ibid.*, p. 224.

29. *From Bed to Worse*, p. 15.

30. "Our Lessons in Auction/by Matilda Stringerley," *Life*, LX (December 5, 1912), 2404.

31. *From Bed to Worse*, p. 152.

32. *My Ten Years in a Quandary*, p. 241. Cf. *ibid.*, pp. 322-24; *The Treasurer's Report*, pp. 174-82. If Benchley were Tennessee Williams, the association of narrator, Negro, and wound might tempt the reckless into retroactive pseudoanalysis.

33. *My Ten Years in a Quandary*, p. 242.

34. Rourke, *American Humor*, p. 89, and *The Roots of American Culture*, Harcourt, Brace (New York, 1942), pp. 270-71. In the latter volume, she claims that "In American humor the sudden extreme of nonsense was new, and the tragic undertone was new."

35. Theodore Strauss, "Colloquy in Queens; Mr. Benchley, Actor, Reflects Sadly on the Fable of Mr. B., the Critic," New York *Times*, February 9, 1941, Sec. 9, p. 5.

36. Harriman, *The Vicious Circle*, pp. 105-106.

37. Edmund Wilson, *A Literary Chronicle* (Garden City, New York, 1956), pp. 54-57. Benchley admired Joe Cook and cared little for the crudities of older vaudeville and supper-club comedians like Weber and Fields. See *The Early Worm*, pp. 148-49.

38. *After 1903—What?*, p. 212. See also Carolyn Wells, "Introduction to *A Nonsense Anthology* (New York, 1958), p. xxviii.

39. Gelett Burgess, "Gelett Burgess as a Humorist," introduction to *The Purple Cow and Other Nonsense,* (New York, 1961), p. viii (a Dover paperback). This self-sketch originally appeared in Thomas L. Masson, ed., *Our American Humorists* (New York, 1922). In the Dover volume (pp. 10-11), the pages of the *Lark* on which the famous quatrain appeared are reproduced. The quatrain is preceded by

> The Purple Cow's Projected Feast:
> Reflections on a Mythic Beast,
> Who's quite Remarkable, at Least.

The animal is drawn charging a rather knobby, scrawny female nude in silhouette that looks like a—deliberately?—bad imitation of Beardsley's fragile females. A file of the *Lark* survives in the Bancroft Library, University of California, Berkeley.

40. Elder, *Ring Lardner*, p. 288.

41. *Obiter Dicta*, I (June, 1913), 38.

42. *From Bed to Worse,* p. 105. Cf. the scholarly non-sequiturs in "Biography by Inches," *Pluck and Luck,* pp. 186-96, also "The Cooper Cycle in American Folk Songs," *20,000 Leagues Under the Sea,* pp. 45-48, and "Men of Harlech!" in *After 1903—What?,* pp. 143-45, in which the satire strikes mainly at the originators, annotators, and renderers of the material—American ballads and Welsh folksongs—rather than at the passive audience or readership.

43. *Life,* LXXVI (December 9, 1920), 1905. There *was* an "Algeciras incident," as Benchley well knew.

44. *The Early Worm,* p. 127.

45. *Chips Off the Old Benchley,* p. xvii.

46. *My Ten Years in a Quandary,* p. 136.

47. *Ibid.,* p. 123.

48. *20,000 Leagues Under the Sea,* p. 192.

49. In a parody of overwritten romances, the smitten lover is advised to "eschew arch glances. For this he was given a small pocket eschewer and ordered to eschew each arch glance thirty-two times." See S. J. Perelman, "In Old Chinatown," cited in E. B. White and Katharine S. White, *A Subtreasury of American Humor,* p. 471. Frank Sullivan's pieces about the "Cliché Expert" likewise turn nonsense into satire-of-nonsense through use of trite material in fresh, incongruous contexts.

50. Wilson, *A Literary Chronicle,* p. 55; Albert Camus, "Franz Kafka," in *The Myth of Sisyphus and Other Essays,* Alfred A. Knopf (Vintage ed., New York, 1960), p. 96.

51. E. g., see "How Long Can You Live?" *After 1903—What?* pp. 217-18.

Chapter Nine

1. By Norman Anthony, *Life,* LX (August 22, 1912), 1937. Cf. "The New Aesop," *Life,* LX (August 1, 1912), 1515, also a drawing in *Mad* magazine (1961) showing Smokey the Bear running from a conflagration; the caption is "Forest Fires Prevent Bears."

2. For a brief discussion of the "Contraries" of an American Indian tribe, see E. Adamson Hoebel, *The Cheyennes* (New York, 1960), pp. 96-97. Cf. George Gascoigne, *The Steel Glass,* lines 383-394, in *Poetry of the English Renaissance,* ed. J. William Hebel and Hoyt H. Hudson (New York, 1930), pp. 98-99.

3. See "The Story of the Bad Little Boy" and "The Story of the Good Little Boy" in *Sketches New and Old. "Sister Mae"* is reprinted

in Jean Shepherd, ed., *The America of George Ade* (New York, 1960), pp. 103-105; cf. "The Patient Toiler Who Got It in the Usual Place," *ibid.*, pp. 217-18.

4. *My Ten Years in a Quandary*, p. 161.

5. These three pieces are in *From Bed to Worse*, pp. 197-200; *No Poems*, pp. 214-19, and *Pluck and Luck*, pp. 231-33, respectively.

6. Other examples of "anti-instructional" parody in Benchley's time were Donald Ogden Stewart, *Perfect Behavior* (New York, 1921)—a parody of Emily Post; Robert Wood, *How to Tell the Birds from the Flowers* (New York, 1917); Fred C. Kelly, *How to Lose Your Money Prudently* (Philadelphia, 1933); and Will Cuppy, *How to Be a Hermit* (New York, 1929), *How to Tell Your Friends From the Apes* (New York, 1931), and *How to Become Extinct* (New York, 1941). This list is far from exhaustive.

7. *Pluck and Luck*, p. 189.

8. *The Treasurer's Report*, p. 82.

9. *My Ten Years in a Quandary*, p. 300.

10. *Ibid.*, p. 295.

11. *No Poems*, pp. 321-22. The first set of dots is mine; the last three sets are Benchley's.

12. "On Being an American," reprinted in *H. L. Mencken Prejudices*, ed. James T. Farrell (New York, 1958), p. 90.

13. *Nathaniel Benchley, op. cit.*, p. 85.

14. *20,000 Leagues Under the Sea*, p. 231.

15. *No Poems*, p. 102.

16. *Ibid.*, p. 244.

17. *Ibid.*, p. 263.

18. *Ibid.*, p. 186.

19. *The Most of S. J. Perelman*, p. 168.

20. *No Poems*, p. 21.

21. *Ibid.*, pp. 93-94.

22. *Ibid.*, p. 120.

23. *Ibid.*, p. 179.

24. *Ibid.*, p. 191.

25. *Ibid.*, pp. 323, 329, 121-29.

26. *After 1903—What?*, pp. 1-7; James Thurber, *The Middle-Aged Man on the Flying Trapeze* (New York and London, 1935), pp. 41-47.

27. Nathaniel Benchley, *op. cit.*, p. 161.

28. *No Poems*, p. 329.

29. *Puck and Luck*, p. 137.

30. *My Ten Years in a Quandary*, p. 284.

31. *Pluck and Luck*, pp. 9-15.

32. *The Benchley Roundup*, p. 313.

33. *Love Conquers All,* pp. 8-12; *Pluck and Luck,* pp. 147-203; *No Poems,* pp. 76-80; *Pluck and Luck,* pp. 268-73; *The Early Worm.* pp. 21-26.

34. Cf. The simile by Sinclair Lewis in *Main Street,* Harcourt, Brace (New York, 1920), p. 33—"The skeleton iron windmill on the farm a few blocks away, at the north end of Main Street, was like the ribs of a dead cow."

35. *Love Conquers All,* pp. 11-12.

36. *Of All Things!,* p. 121.

37. *From Bed to Worse,* p. 257.

38. *My Ten Years in a Quandary,* p. 25.

39. *Ibid.,* p. 142.

40. Martin Esslin, *The Theatre of the Absurd* (Garden City, New York), p. 245; Christian Morgenstern, *Alle Galgenlieder* (Wiesbaden, 1947), p. 38.

41. *The Treasurer's Report,* pp. 47-52.

42. *No Poems,* p. 283.

43. *20,000 Leagues Under the Sea,* p. 206. The brackets in the second excerpt are Benchley's.

44. *The Benchley Roundup,* p. 315.

45. *After 1903—What?,* p. 259.

46. *My Ten Years in a Quandary,* p. 123.

47. *Ibid.,* p. 338.

48. *Ibid.,* p. 329. The piece ends with "This fragment of manuscript was found floating in a bather off Santa Barbara."

49. Ring Lardner, "Sit Still," in *A Subtreasury of American Humor,* pp. 486-89; James Thurber, "The Whip-poor-will," *Alarms and Diversions* (New York, 1957), pp. 307-14; "Nesselrode to Jeopardy," *The Most of S. J. Perelman,* pp. 487-94.

50. *The Autobiography of Will Rogers,* p. 248.

Chapter Ten

1. George S. Chappell, *Through the Alimentary Canal with Gun and Camera* (New York, 1958). In this paperbound reissue of the 1930 original, Chappell's acknowledgement of indebtedness to Benchley may be found on pp. vi-ix, and Benchley's tongue-in-cheek disclaimer in Robert's "Introduction," p. v.

2. Nathaniel Benchley, *op. cit.,* p. 74.

3. *Ibid.,* p. 45.

4. *Ibid.,* p. 73.

5. Burton Rascoe, "What of Our Essayists?" *Bookman,* LV (March, 1922), 74-75. In addition to *Of All Things!* Rascoe reviewed Colby, *The Margin of Hesitation;* Day, *The Crow's Nest;* Strunsky, *Sinbad*

and His Friends, Morley, *Plum Pudding;* Beerbohm, *And Even Now,* and James Huneker, *Variations.*

6. Anon., "Quips and Capers of Our Court Fools," New York *Times Book Review,* January 14, 1923, p. 2. The review also deals with volumes by Ade, Thomas L. Masson, Adams, Marquis, and others.

7. E. L. Pearson, Springfield, Massachusetts, *Republican,* December 28, 1921, p. 8.

8. Gilbert Seldes, *Dial,* LXXII (January, 1922), 95; Edmund Wilson, Jr., "Mr. Benchley's Message to His Age" *New Republic,* XXX (March 29, 1922), 150.

9. Edmund Wilson, "The Scarsdale Aristotle," *Bookman,* LVI (January, 1923), 636-37. Cf. Lawrence Mason, *Literary Review* (January 6, 1923), 363, where *Love Conquers All* is criticized for having "too many essays of the routine, stereotyped, machine-made order," but praised for "cheerful effrontery, riotous high spirits and monstrous fertility in preposterous invention." Thirty-seven years after Wilson had first wished that Benchley were "more savage" and more sweeping, a British reviewer felt that the best American humorists were more savage and tough-minded than their British colleagues. See Roy Perrott, "Through Storm-Tossed Seas of Humour," Manchester *Guardian,* December 17, 1959—an essay-review of *The Most of S. J. Perelman.*

10. John Farrar, "The Latest Laugh," *Bookman,* LXII (February, 1926), 713-14—a review of *Pluck and Luck.* See also William Rose Benét, "Benchley's Desperate Remedy," *SRL,* XVII (January 8, 1938), 7.

11. Frank Sullivan, "Introduction" to *Chips Off the Old Benchley,* pp. xvii, xix; James Thurber, *Credos and Curios,* pp. 149, 150; Dorothy Parker, "Introduction" to *The Most of S. J. Perelman,* p. xii.

12. Esslin, *The Theatre of the Absurd,* p. 247.

13. E. B. Thompson, of King Features Syndicate, to Norris W. Yates, January 17, 1964. Many pieces from this column reappeared in *My Ten Years in a Quandary* and in *After 1903—What?*

14. R. W. Hager, of Harper & Row, to Norris W. Yates, March 13, 1964. The four volumes are: *Inside Benchley; Benchley Beside Himself; The Benchley Roundup; Chips Off the Old Benchley.* Blair, *Horse Sense in American Humor* (Chicago, 1943), p. 280, says that Benchley's books had sold a total of 120,000 by 1942. Neither source includes the sales of *The Benchley Roundup* in the Delta paperbound edition (1962). Margaret Case Harriman, while writing *The Vicious Circle* (1951) found that certain students at Princeton "had read all of Woollcott, Benchley, and Parker. 'And I'll tell you one thing,' said another boy, 'there's nobody writing today, except Thurber, who can touch them'" (p. 299).

15. *Ibid.,* p. 59; Dorothy Parker, as cited in the Des Moines, Iowa, *Sunday Register,* October 13, 1963, p. 4-W. Mrs. Harriman, a successful writer, is also the daughter of Frank Case, who managed the Algonquin during its great days and eventually owned it.

16. *Ibid.,* p. 5. I have relied on this book for most of the factual material about the Round Table, but see also Samuel Hopkins Adams, *A. Woollcott, His Life and His World* (New York, 1945), pp. 118-27.

17. *Ibid.,* p. 221.

18. *Ibid.,* p. 66.

19. Adams, *A. Woollcott,* p. 121. According to Adams, Benchley and Frank Sullivan were credited by the press with so many humorous sayings that their bosses invited them to " 'save it for home use.' "

20. Elder, *Ring Lardner,* p. 283.

21. Robert Benchley, "Author's Note," *The Treasurer's Report,* p. 334. Mrs. Harriman in *The Vicious Circle* (p. 88) merely mentions that one night at Neysa McMein's, Robert "entertained his friends" with this monologue. The program of *No Siree!,* the occasion when the "Report" was first given publicly, is reprinted in *The Vicious Circle,* pp. 89-97.

22. *Ibid.,* p. 175.

23. However, Marquis was influenced by Adams, as were most other newspaper columnists of the time. See James Gray, "The Journalist as Literary Man," in May Brodbeck, James Gray, and Walter Metzger, *American Non-Fiction 1900-1950* (Chicago, 1952), p. 141, and Edward Anthony, *O Rare Don Marquis* (Garden City, New York, 1962), p. 138.

24. In supporting this view, one may quote Benchley against himself. He claimed that *The New Yorker* had "revolutionized the illustrated joke," replacing "the old feeble two-line joke" with a fresh and infinitely more civilized form—the "illustrated single remark." Max Eastman refutes Benchley by showing that the old *Masses* had used many more one-line captions than captions of two lines or more. The *Masses* was founded in 1911 and Eastman became editor in 1912. See *Enjoyment of Laughter,* pp. 90-91.

25. *The Vicious Circle,* pp. 179-80.

26. *The Years with Ross,* pp. 22-24. Thurber's statement casts doubt on Mrs. Harriman's comment in *The Vicious Circle* (p. 181) that, "At first *The New Yorker* was written largely by members of the Round Table and their friends, anonymously or under pen names."

27. *The Years with Ross,* p. 35.

28. *Ibid.,* p. 25.

29. Cuppy was five years older than Benchley, but much younger as a writer of humor. His first book, *How to Be a Hermit,* appeared during the same year as *Is Sex Necessary?,* the first prose in book

form by Thurber and White. That year, 1929, the stock market crashed.

30. *Credos and Curios*, p. 149. The pieces referred to by Thurber are "The First Pigeon of Spring," *Chips Off the Old Benchley*, pp. 232-33; " 'He Travels Fastest—'," *Ibid.*, pp. 47-51; " 'Take the Witness!' " *My Ten Years in a Quandary*, pp. 4-9, and possibly "Down with Pigeons," *From Bed to Worse*, pp. 275-82. Also "French News," in *The Treasurer's Report*, pp 157-65, from which the quotation about cuts is taken (p. 159), though Benchley was referring to *Le Matin* rather than *L'Éclaireur*.

31. *Credos and Curios*, p. 148.

32. Nathaniel Benchley, *op. cit.*, pp. 17-18.

33. *Ibid.*, pp. 256-58, where the movie shorts in which Robert Benchley participated are listed. Benchley also played in many full-length feature films, including *Nice Girl, Foreign Correspondent*, and *The Reluctant Dragon*.

34. *Ibid.*, p. 252.

35. "The Theatre," *The New Yorker*, VI (December 20, 1930), 32. His comment was especially apt because this actor was currently playing the Angel Gabriel in *Green Pastures*. For tributes to Benchley, see anon., "Robert Benchley," *The New Yorker*, XXI (December 1, 1945), 138; "Robert Benchley," *Newsweek*, XXVI (December 3, 1945), 90, and "The One and Only Benchley," *Reader's Digest*, XLVIII (February, 1946), 27.

Selected Bibliography

PRIMARY SOURCES

Books by Benchley

After 1903—What? New York and London: Harper & Brothers, 1938.

Benchley Beside Himself. New York and London: Harper and Brothers, 1943. A selection of pieces reprinted from earlier books.

Benchley—or Else! New York and London: Harper and Brothers, 1947. Selections reprinted from earlier books.

The Benchley Roundup, a Selection by Nathaniel Benchley of His Favorites. New York: Harper & Brothers, 1954. Compiled by the son of Robert Benchley from Robert's previous books.

Chips Off the Old Benchley. New York: Harper & Brothers, 1949. "Introduction" by Frank Sullivan. A compilation by Gertrude Darling Benchley (widow of Robert), largely from previously unreprinted material.

The Early Worm. New York: Henry Holt, 1927.

From Bed to Worse; or, Comforting Thoughts About the Bison. New York and London: Harper & Brothers, 1934.

Inside Benchley. New York and London: Harper & Brothers, 1942. Selections from earlier books.

Love Conquers All. New York: Henry Holt, 1922.

My Ten Years in a Quandary, and How They Grew. New York and London: Harper & Brothers, 1936.

No Poems; or, Around the World Backwards and Sideways. New York and London: Harper & Brothers, 1932.

Of All Things! New York: Henry Holt, 1921.

Pluck and Luck. New York: Henry Holt, 1925.

The "Reel" Benchley; Robert Benchley at His Hilarious Best in Pictures. New York: Wyn, 1950. "Foreword" by Howard Dietz. Photographs and quotations from films in which Benchley participated.

The Treasurer's Report, and Other Aspects of Community Singing. New York and London: Harper & Brothers, 1930.

20,000 Leagues Under the Sea; or, David Copperfield. New York: Henry Holt, 1928. (In 1924, Benchley dropped the middle initial from his name; thus, his name appears in *Of All Things!* and *Love Conquers All* as Robert C. Benchley. Thereafter, it appears as Robert Benchley. The same change may be noticed if one compares short pieces written before and after late August or early September, 1924.)

Selected unreprinted pieces by Benchley (exclusive of those in *Obiter Dicta*—much of which was written by him anonymously—and in his columns: "Books and Other Things" in the New York *World,* "Drama" in *Life,* and "The Wayward Press" and "The Theatre" in *The New Yorker*).

Untitled editorial, Harvard *Lampoon,* LXI (April 13, 1911), 126-27.
Untitled editorial, *Lampoon,* LXI (May 24, 1911), 183.
Untitled editorial, *Lampoon,* LXI (June 22, 1911), 271.
Untitled editorial, *Lampoon,* LXII (October 21, 1911), 45.
Untitled editorial, *Lampoon,* LXII (November 24, 1911), 151.
Untitled editorial, *Lampoon,* LXII (December 21, 1911), 262-63.
"All About Relativity," *Vanity Fair,* XIV (March, 1920), 61.
"America's Greatest Movement: the Jaw Movement," *World Outlook,* II (October, 1916), 8-9.
"Barnum and the Birth Rate," *Forum,* LXX (July, 1923), 1742-47.
"Beginning a Sort of Department," *Bookman,* LXVI (November, 1927), 267-69.
"Blurbs," *Forum,* LXX (December, 1923), 2243-46.
"Brave Illusion," *Collier's,* LXIX (May 20, 1922), 11.
"A Breath from the Pines," *Life,* LXXVIII (October 6, 1921), 22, 29.
"Bring Needle Beer Back," *The New Yorker,* IX (April 22, 1933), 12.
"The 'Coupla Drinks' Myth," *Collier's,* LXX (July 1, 1922 , 8.
"Design for Revolution," *The New Yorker,* IX (February 25, 1933), 17-18.
"Dialectic Hint on How to Win an Argument," *Life,* LXXVI (December 9, 1920), 1095.
"Do Flowers Cheat?" *Life,* LXXXVI (August 13, 1925), 18.
"The Doodlebugs," *Lampoon* (December, 1954), 10-11.
"Drama, What Big Teeth You Have!" *Bookman,* LXIX (June, 1929), 387-89.
"Elementary Economics," *Life,* LXXVI (September 23, 1920), 5, 32-33.
"The Emancipation Proclamation, If It Had Been Written and Delivered from the Front Porch at Marion, Ohio," *Life,* LXXVI (September 9, 1920), 449.
"The Famous Fuie Tapestry, Fortunately Just Stolen," *Life,* LXXXIII (November 4, 1926), 9.
"The Fate of the Funny Men," *Bookman,* LVII (June, 1923), 455-57.
"Football Phenomena," *Collier's,* LVI (November 20, 1915), 32.
"Foreword" to S. J. Perelman, *Strictly from Hunger.* New York:

Simon and Schuster, 1937.

"Force of Habit," *The New Yorker*, III (August 3, 1927), 19.

"Glorifying the American Flea," *Bookman*, LXVII (March, 1928), 64-66.

(with E. L. McKinney) "The Harvard Lampoon Sewing Circle," "Hamlet for Broadway," *Vanity Fair*, V (January, 1916), 67.

"Have You a Little German Agent in Your Home?", *Vanity Fair*, X (March, 1918), 51, 106. Under pseudonym "Brighton Perry." *Lampoon*, LXI (May 6, 1911), 153.

"Have You Tried These New Memory Courses?" *Vanity Fair*, XII (June, 1919), 52.

"Heroes of Realism," *Bookman*, LII (February, 1921), 559-60.

"Hints on Writing a Book," *Vanity Fair* (October, 1914), 41.

"Home for the Holidays!" *The New Yorker*, IX (March 25, 1933), 15-16.

"How I Make People Like Me," *Vanity Fair*, XIII (January, 1920), 31.

"Ideal Tax Tours," *Life*, LXXXII (July 12, 1923), 24.

"The Ideal Tour, What You Plan to Do and What You Do," *Life*, LXXXIX (April 7, 1927), 33.

"Introduction" to George S. Chappell, *Through the Alimentary Canal with Gun and Camera*. New York: Dover, 1963 (first edition, New York: Frederick A Stokes, 1930), v.

"Ivy Oration," Harvard *Advocate* (June, 1912), reprinted in *The Harvard "Advocate" Anthology*. New York: Twayne, 1950, pp. 128-34.

"*Life's* Current Events Class," *Life*, LXXVIII (October 13, 1921), 3.

"*Life's* Old Print Collection," *Life*, LXXIII (August 14, 1924), 13.

" 'The Lottery Man' at the Majestic Theatre," Harvard *Advocate* (March, 1911), repr. in *The Harvard "Advocate" Anthology*, ed. Donald Hall. New York: Twayne, 1950, pp. 127-28.

"The Low-Down on the Big Fight, Based on a Visit to the Opposing Camps," *Life*, LXXXVIII (September 23, 1926), 9.

"Making Grammar Popular," *The New Yorker*, IX (May 20, 1933), 20.

"The Making of a Red," *Nation*, CVIII (March 15, 1919), 399-400.

"Minutes in the Courses, III, History," *Lampoon*, LXI (May 24, 1911), 188.

"Mr. Benchley's Reply to Mr. Ritchie of Seattle," *Life*, LXCI (May 31, 1928), 11, 19.

"Mr. Vanity Fair," *Bookman*, L (January, 1920), 429-33. Under pseudonym "Brighton Perry."

"A Nation's Tribute, Cross-Section of a Hero's Mail from Disinterested Admirers," *Life*, LXXXIX (June 16, 1927), 7.

"Of Indoor Sports," *Collier's*, LVI (January 8, 1916), 81.
"The Official Yachting Cap," *The New Yorker*, III (June 18, 1927), 38.
"Our Own Straw Vote," *Life*, XCII (October 19, 1928), 4-5.
"Out Front," *Harper's Magazine*, CLII (March, 1926), 477-82.
" 'Please Do Not Flout Natural Laws'," *The New Yorker*, VI (May 17, 1930), 23.
"A Possible Revolution in Hollywood," *Yale Review*, n. s., XXI (September, 1931), 100-110.
"Price-Slashing, What You Read in the Papers," *Life*, LXXVI (October 21, 1920), 708.
"Retrospect," *Life*, LXXXIX (April 28, 1927), 6.
"The Revolt of the Seers—Off," *The New Yorker*, III (August 20, 1927), 24.
"Robert Charles Benchley," *Harvard College Class of 1912. Twenty-Fifth Anniversary Report*. Cambridge, Massachusetts: Cosmos Press, 1937, pp. 41-43 (an autobiographical sketch).
"The Silent Art of Joe Jackson," *Everybody's Magazine*, XLIV (February, 1921), 30-31.
"The Street of Broken Hearts," *Life*, LXXVIII (December 22, 1921), 20.
"Time Out," *Bookman*, LXVI (January, 1928), 552-54.
"To Open—Press Here," *Life*, LXXVI (November 4, 1920), 812-13.
"Training the Moving-Vanguard," *Life*, LXXVI (October 7, 1920), 633.
"The Unsung Heroes," *The New Yorker*, III (June 18, 1927), 22.
"Up the Dark Stairs—", *The New Yorker*, I (December 19, 1925), 7-8.
"Vacation Trunks," *Life*, LXXVI (September 16, 1920), 518.
"A Warning," *The New Yorker*, VIII (July 2, 1932), 13-14.
"Where Are My Skates?" *Bookman*, LXVI (December, 1927), 415-17.
"The Will to Suffer," *Bellman*, XXII (March 17, 1917), 297-98.
" 'Your Loving Son, Nora Bayes'," *Everybody's Magazine*, XLIV (May, 1921), 52-53.

SELECTIVE SECONDARY SOURCES

Books and Articles about Benchley

ALLEN, FREDERICK LEWIS. "Robert Charles Benchley," *Harvard College Class of 1912, Thirty-Fifth Anniversary Report*. Cambridge, Massachusetts: Cosmos Press, 1947. Reminiscences by a friend and fellow-humorist who became an eminent editor and historian.
Anon. "Benchley," in "Talk of the Town," *The New Yorker*, XXI (January 5, 1946), 18-19. Rich collection of anecdotes.

Anon. "Bob Benchley Dies; Noted Humorist, 56," New York *Times*, November 22, 1945, p. 35. Brief obituary.

Anon. "The Jester Lives On," *Newsweek*, XLVI (November 7, 1955), 120. Review of Nathaniel Benchley, *Robert Benchley*.

Anon. "Milestones," *Time*, XLVI (December 3, 1945), 72. Death notice that erroneously ascribes to Benchley the quip about wet clothes and a dry martini.

Anon. "Money for Minutes," Time, XXXII (September 19, 1938), 46-51. Includes comment on Benchley's first regular radio program.

Anon. "The One and Only Benchley," *Reader's Digest*, XLVIII (February, 1946), 27. Anecdotes from writings by Leonard Lyons, Frank Sullivan, and the New York *World-Telegram*. One anecdote also concerns Donald Ogden Stewart, and one, James Thurber.

Anon. "Quips and Capers of Our Court Fools," New York *Times Book Review*, January 14, 1923, p. 2. Review of *Of All Things!* and of new humor by other authors.

Anon. "Robert Benchley: 1889-1945," *Newsweek*, XXVI (December 3, 1945), 90. Obituary notice.

Anon. "Robert (Charles) Benchley," *Current Biography, 1941.* New York: H. W. Wilson, 1941, pp. 63-65.

BENCHLEY, NATHANIEL. "Birds, Beasts, and Benchley," *Good Housekeeping*, CXXVII (November, 1948), 187-90. This item and the two following were incorporated into the same author's *Robert Benchley*.

————. "Bon-Voyage Benchley," *Holiday*, XV (June, 1954), 83-86.

————. "Businessman Benchley," *Holiday*, XVII (March, 1955), 73-76.

————. *Robert Benchley, a Biography.* New York: McGraw-Hill, 1955. By Robert's eldest son, a novelist, playwright, and short-story writer. Well-written and more reliable than the average "authorized" biography.

BENCHLEY, ROBERT. "Robert Charles Benchley," *Harvard College Class of 1912, Twenty-fifth Anniversary Report.* Cambridge, Massachusetts: Cosmos Press, 1937, pp. 41-43. This humorous autobiographical sketch is inaccurate in some details.

BENET, WILLIAM ROSE. "Benchley's Desperate Remedy," *Saturday Review of Literature*, XVII (January 8, 1938), 7. Review of *After 1903—What?*

————. "The Phoenix Nest," *idem*, XXVIII (December 15, 1945), 31-32. Reminiscences; appreciation of his "cuckoo" humor.

BLAIR, WALTER. *Horse Sense in American Humor, from Benjamin Franklin to Ogden Nash.* Chicago: University of Chicago, 1942. Placement of Benchley, Thurber, and Perelman in relation to earlier American humor. Perhaps too much emphasis on them as "crazy men" in an otherwise cogent survey.

————. *Native American Humor*. San Francisco: Chandler, 1960. Brief treatment of Benchley and other "neurotic" modern humorists has been added to the 1937 version of this standard text.

BROWN, JOHN MASON. "High Spirits in the Twenties," *Horizon*, IV (July, 1962), 33-41. Biographical details about Benchley and other "characters."

BRYAN, III, J. "Funny Man, a Study in Professional Frustration," *Saturday Evening Post*, CCXII (September 23, 1939), 10-11, 93-94, 96-97; (October 7, 1939), 32, 65-68, 70, 72. Mainly about Benchley's life in Hollywood, especially at the "Garden of Allah" apartments. Should be used with caution.

DAUGHERTY, FRANK. "Benchley in Films 15 Years; Started by Writing Titles," *Christian Science Monitor*, July 26, 1940, p. 12. Interview with Benchley about his movie career.

DEVOTO, BERNARD. "The Lineage of Eustace Tilley," *Saturday Review of Literature*, XVI (September 25, 1937), 4-5, 20. Finds parallel between humor by Max Adeler (Charles Heber Clark) and "The Treasurer's Report."

"The Editors." "Robert Benchley," *The New Yorker*, XXI (December 1, 1945), 138. Brief summing-up of Benchley as critic, writer, and person.

FARRAR, JOHN. "The Latest Laugh," *Bookman*, LXII (February, 1926), 713-14. Review of *Pluck and Luck* stressing philosophical element in Benchley's humor.

FULLER, JOHN G. "Trade Winds," *Saturday Review*, XLVI (April 20, 1963), 8, 10. Reminiscences of Benchley at Harvard as told to author by the distinguished economist, Clarence B. Randall.

GIBBS, WOLCOTT. "Robert Benchley: In Memoriam," New York *Times Book Review*, December 16, 1945, p. 3. Critical evaluation, biographical details, and anecdotes by friend and fellow-humorist.

MASON, LAWRENCE. Review of *Love Conquers All* in *Literary Review*, January 6, 1923, p. 363. Criticizes book for having "too many essays of the routine, stereotyped, machine-made order," but otherwise favorable.

MASSON, THOMAS L. *Our American Humorists*. New York: Moffat, Yard, 1922, pp. 47-52. Humorous biographical sketch. Followed by "The Social Life of the Newt."

MILLER, WILLIAM LEE. "There Really Was a Benchley," *Reporter*, XIV (January 12, 1956), 39. Essay-review of Nathaniel Benchley, *Robert Benchley*. Claims that Benchley's humor included little social indignation.

O'HARA, JOHN. "Appointment with O'Hara," *Collier's*, CXXXVII (January 6, 1956), 6. Insights concerning Benchley "as a person and a personality."

————. "Thisa and Thata," *Newsweek*, XVIII (July 21, 1941), 54. Rhapsodic tribute.

PEARSON, E. L. Review of *Of All Things!* and other humor, Springfield (Massachusetts) *Republican*, December 28, 1921, p. 8. Thinks Benchley may replace Artemus Ward, Mr. Dooley, and other crackerbox humorists.

PORTER, AMY. "Garden of Allah I Love You," *Collier's*, CXX (November 22, 1947), 18-19, 102, 105. On Benchley's life in Hollywood. Should be used cautiously.

RASCOE, BURTON. "What of Our Essayists?" *Bookman*, LV (March, 1922), 74-75. Review of *Of All Things!* and of other humor. Claims American familiar essayists are superior to British.

SHERWOOD, ROBERT E. "Foreword" to Nathaniel Benchley, *Robert Benchley*. New York: McGraw-Hill, 1955, xiii-xvi. Stresses many-sidedness of Benchey's humor and personality. One of the best brief interpretations.

SELDES, GILBERT. Review of *Of All Things!* in *Dial*, LXXII (January, 1922), 95. Stresses satire of business, press, theater.

STEWART, DONALD OGDEN. "Mr. Humor," *Nation*, CLXXIX (October 16, 1954), 343. Review of *The Benchley Roundup*.

STRAUSS, THEODORE. "Colloquy in Queens, Mr. Benchley, Actor, Reflects Sadly on the Fate of Mr. Benchley, the Critic," New York *Times*, February 9, 1941, Sec. 9, p. 5. Interview in which Benchley tells how he became an actor.

STRUNSKY, ROBERT. "The Benchley Case," *Saturday Review of Literature*, XIV (May 9, 1936), 10. Review of *My Ten Years in a Quandary*.

SUGRUE, THOMAS. "The Infralabialis Art of Mr. Benchley," *Saturday Review of Literature*, XXVI, (July 10, 1943), 20. Review of *Benchley Beside Himself*. Sees Benchley as a window into social history, 1919-1939.

SULLIVAN, FRANK. "A Friend Is Grateful That Bob Benchley Chose This Age to Live In," *PM*, November 27, 1945, p. 21.

————. "Bob Benchley . . . Knight of Wonderful Nonsense," *Senior Scholastic*, XLVIII (February 25, 1946), 14. Reprint of *PM* article.

————. "Introduction." *Chips Off the Old Benchley*. New York: Harper & Brothers, 1949. Stresses sanity and integrity of Benchley's narrator.

THURBER, JAMES. "The Incomparable Mr. Benchley," New York *Times Book Review*, September 18, 1949, pp. 1, 31. Essay-review of

Chips; revised as a more general appreciation and reprinted in *Credos and Curios.* New York and Evanston: Harper & Row, 1962, pp. 146-52. Both versions stress the liveliness of Benchley's style and his influence on the author.

WILSON, EDMUND, JR. "Mr. Benchley's Message to His Age," *New Republic,* XXX (March 29, 1922), 150. Review of *Of All Things!* Stresses that Benchley is leader of a new group of satirists, and criticizes him for not satirizing business more whole-heartedly.

————. "The Scarsdale Aristotle," *Bookman,* LVI (January, 1923), 636-37. Floridly humorous review of *Love Conquers All.*

————. *A Literary Chronicle: 1920-1950.* Garden City, New York: Doubleday, 1956, pp. 49-65. Written in 1924, this includes comment on the recent growth of nonsense humor.

WINTERICH, JOHN T. "The Benchley Boom," *Saturday Review of Literature,* XV (December 26, 1936), 19.

————. "The Wistful Wag," *Saturday Review,* XXXVIII (December 10, 1955), 13-14. Review of Nathaniel Benchley, *Robert Benchley.*

YATES, NORRIS W. "Robert Benchley's Normal Bumbler," *The American Humorist: Conscience of the Twentieth Century.* Ames, Iowa: Iowa State University, 1964. Stresses the sanity of Benchley's humor and the sound values embodied in the author's alter ego.

Books and Articles Useful in the Study of Benchley and His Background

Anon. "The Gossip Shop," *Bookman,* LXII (December, 1925), 523. Includes biographical comment on Benchley and his peers in humor.

Anon. "A Meeting of President Will Rogers' Cabinet," *Life,* XCII (November 16, 1928), 33-36. Material on the campaign of the Anti-Bunk Party.

Anon. "No Satire," *Life,* LXXIV (September 18, 1919), 498. Suggests that Americans will not tolerate satire because their environment changes too fast and because "so many Americans are satires in themselves."

BECKER, STEPHEN. *Comic Art in America.* New York: Simon and Schuster, 1959. Surveys humor of the comic strip and cartoon, with emphasis on the twentieth century.

BRIDGEMAN, RICHARD. *The Colloquial Style in America.* New York: Oxford University Press, 1966. Includes much about the influence of common speech on the writings of selected influential fictioneers.

CLEATON, IRENE, AND ALLEN CLEATON. *Books and Battles*. Boston: Houghton, Mifflin, 1937. On censorship of American literature, 1920-1930.

COLBY, FRANK MOORE. "Humor," in Harold Stearns (ed.), *Civilization in the United States*. New York: Harcourt, Brace, 1922, pp. 463-66. Survey of the field by a practicing master of the "light" essay.

CONNELLY, MARC. "The Most Unforgettable Character I've Met," *Reader's Digest*, LXXXVI (May, 1965), 72-78. Mainly anecdotal, with a few anecdotes not available elsewhere.

DE MOTT, BENJAMIN. "The New Irony: Sickniks and Others," *American Scholar*, XXXI (Winter, 1961-1962), 108-19. The postulate of an elite of good men is at least a century old in humor; however, the "sick" humor of the 1950's implies that the assumptions of this elite were shaken.

DESMOND, ROBERT W. "Something to Think About," *Christian Science Monitor Weekly Magazine Section*, August 17, 1938, pp. 4, 14. Concerning film "shorts."

ESSLIN, MARTIN. *The Theatre of the Absurd*. Garden City, New York: Doubleday, 1961. Pp. 241-47 include a good brief survey of verbal nonsense humor in Europe and America.

GURKO, LEO. *The Angry Decade*. New York: Dodd, Mead, 1947. Political, social, literary trends and tastes in the 1930's.

HILL, HAMLIN. "Modern American Humor: the Janus Laugh," *College English*, XXV (December, 1963), 170-76.

KLAPP, ORRIN E. *Heroes, Villains, and Fools, the Changing American Character*. Englewood Cliffs, New Jersey: Prentice-Hall, 1962. Sees five kinds of "American fools" in the popular mind: incompetents, debunkers, nonconformists, over-conformists, and certain hard-to-classify types (especially the comic butt and the clever fool) as having "conspicuous functions as outlets for aggressive tension."

KRONENBERGER, LOUIS. "The American Sense of Humor," *Company Manners, a Cultural Inquiry into American Life*. New York: Mentor, 1955. Makes distinction between satire (a creation of the minority), and humor of a sort used mainly by the masses to disguise themselves to themselves.

LEACOCK, STEPHEN. *Humor and Humanity: an Introduction to the Study of Humor*. New York: Henry Holt, 1938. One of the two books about humor by a humorist whose influence on Benchley was considerable. Basic position: "Humor and human kindliness are one."

MACY, JOHN. Review of Wallace Irwin, *Letters of a Japanese Schoolboy*, in *Bookman*, XXIX (May, 1909), 311-12. Predicts that "the next satirist, who will be due in about ten years," will have need of "a voice and a lingo" equal to those of Dooley and Togo.

MARX, LEO. "The Vernacular Tradition in American Literature." *Studies in American Culture.* Ed. Joseph J. Kwiatt and Mary C. Turpie. Minneapolis: University of Minnesota Press, 1960. Cogent discussion of how "common" language was developed by Whitman, Twain, and others into a medium for literary expression despite its anti-intellectual tendency.

NUMASWAWA, KOJI. "Our Funny Men: an Examination of Contemporary American Humorists," *Hiyoshi Faculty Review* (Autumn, 1963), 29-52. Mostly about Thurber and the sanity behind his guise of " 'vague little man.' "

O'CONNOR, WILLIAM VAN. *The Grotesque: an American Genre and Other Essays.* Carbondale, Illinois: Southern Illinois University Press, 1962. In the title essay, the grotesque in American fiction is defined as the abnormal which has become normal. The definition invites application to American humor in verse and in essays.

PETT, SAUL. "Dorothy's 70—and Still Sharp," Des Moines (Iowa) *Sunday Register,* Sec. 6, pp. 1-W, 4-W. Wire-service interview which may have had different headlines elsewhere. Tart reminiscences about the Algonquin Round Table and other matters.

REXROTH, KENNETH. "The Decline of American Humor," *Nation,* CLXXIV (April, 1957), 374-76. Denunciation, by an elder statesman of the "beatniks," of the humor encouraged by *The New Yorker.* Calls this humor a commercialized, unrealistic product made by and for the new leisure class.

ROGERS, WILL. "I Accept the Nomination," *Life,* XCI (May 31, 1928), 3. Agrees to run on ticket of Anti-Bunk Party.

SELDES, GILBERT. *The Seven Lively Arts.* New York and London: Harper, 1924. Valuable material and commentary about the theater, movies, comic strips, popular music, and humor of the early 1920's.

Index

Index